Margaret.

This book brought you to mind with your memory walks on the Lagan Towpath. I hope you enjoy.

Lillian
x

My Lagan Love

~ A Portrait of the River Lagan ~

Paintings by Gillian Lutton

Text by Ian Hill

Cottage Publications

First published by Cottage Publications,
an imprint of Laurel Cottage Ltd.
Donaghadee, N. Ireland 2008.
Copyrights Reserved.
© Illustrations by Gillian Lutton 2008.
© Text by Ian Hill 2007.
All rights reserved.
No part of this book may be reproduced or stored on any media
without the express written permission of the publishers.
Design & Origination in Northern Ireland.
Printed & bound in China.
ISBN 978 1 900935 65 4

Ian Hill, who can trace his ancestors, the Guinnesses, the Hills and the McCartans, back to the 16th century banks of the Lagan, is product of Enniskillen's minor Public School Portora Royal, redbrick Queen's University, London's Royal College of Surgeons and Austria's then CIA-funded Salzburg Seminar in American Studies.

An anatomist seduced by the media's charms, Ian filed copy as critic and commentator – as he still does – for newspapers and journals, radio and television stations, in Belfast, Dublin and London before becoming a Director of the Northern Ireland Tourist Board.

Currently sitting on the Historic Buildings Council, the Historic Monuments Council, the Joint Council for Industrial Heritage, plus the Boards of the Northern Ireland Museums Council, the Cathedral Quarter Arts Festival, Downpatrick's Opera Fringe, Wexford Opera's Dumbworld Project and the Ulster Orchestra, Ian also represents Ireland on L'Association Internationale des Critiques de Théâtre.

This, Ian's second book for Cottage Publications following on *Lecale – St Patrick's County Down*, is his sixteenth Irish travel book for publishers based in Belfast, Dublin, London, Paris and New York.

Banbridge born artist Gillian Lutton began painting in 1989 and over the last 18 years has held eleven very successful exhibitions of her work. She has also had paintings exhibited and sold in Royal Ulster Academy exhibitions in the Ulster Museum and, in 1996, illustrated *Banbridge – An Illustrated History and Companion for Cottage Publications*.

Gillian took a break from painting while she devoted most of her time to her two young daughters, but returned with an incredibly successful exhibition in November 2006 before being commissioned by Cottage Publications to provide the illustrations in early 2007 for the acclaimed first title in this series, *By the Banks of the Bann*.

Gillian's work clearly demonstrates her passion for the countryside in which she lives. Her paintings convey a real sense of time and place through her creative use of light, shade and subtle colour.

Gillian's painting can best be described as both instinctive and intuitive. Her recent paintings have brought a new maturity and sensitivity to her work, in which her skill of going to the essence of her subject, exploring and responding to the spirit of each place, is very apparent.

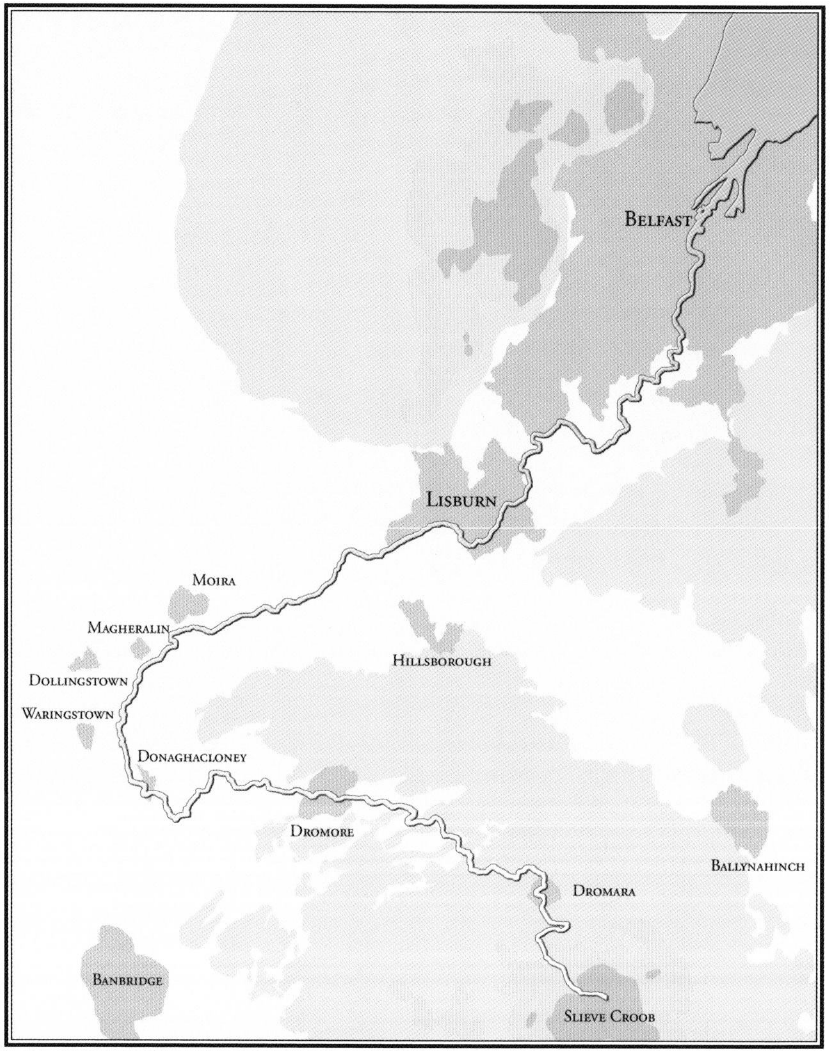

BELFAST

LISBURN

MOIRA

MAGHERALIN

HILLSBOROUGH

DOLLINGSTOWN

WARINGSTOWN

DONAGHACLONEY

DROMORE

BALLYNAHINCH

DROMARA

BANBRIDGE

SLIEVE CROOB

Contents and Illustrations

My Lagan Love

Where Lagan stream sings lullaby
There blows a lily fair;
The twilight gleam is in her eye
The night is on her hair
And like a love-sick leanán-sidhe
She has my heart in thrall
Nor life I owe, nor liberty
For Love is lord of all.

Her father sails a running-barge
'Twixt Lambeg and The Drum;
And on the lonely river-marge
She clears his hearth for him.
When she was only fairy-high
Her gentle mother died;
But dew-love keeps her memory
Green on the Lagan side.

And often when the beetle's horn
Hath lulled the eve to sleep
I steal unto her shieling lorn
And thro' the dooring peep.
There on the cricket's singing-stone,
She spares the bogwood fire,
And hums in sad, sweet, undertone
The songs of heart's desire

Her welcome, like her love for me,
Is from her heart within:
Her warm kiss is felicity
That knows no taint of sin.
And, when I stir my foot to go,
'Tis leaving Love and light
To feel the wind of longing blow
From out the dark of night.

Where Lagan stream sings lullaby,
There blows a lily fair;
The twilight gleam is in her eye
The night is on her hair
And like a love-sick leanán-sidhe
She has my heart in thrall
Nor life I owe nor liberty
For Love is lord of all.

These lyrics to *My Lagan Love* are by Joseph Campbell, known also as *Seosamh MacCathmhaoil*, written to a traditional melody collected in 1903 as *The Belfast Maid* by ethnomusicologist Herbert Hughes.

Today there are salmon, grey mullett, flounders and lampreys in the mouth of the Lagan – and brown trout near its source on Slieve Croob. Yet this grey-brown river which sluices through Belfast is not one of Europe's great rivers, a mere trickle when compared, say, to the Danube, the Rhine, the Seine or the Thames. But, now cleaner than it has been for centuries, its flow once created the power to run the mills and foundries, not just of the cities of Belfast and Lisburn, but of every town and village from the mountains to the sea, thus establishing much of the wealth of Ulster, Ireland's northernmost province.

After the Thaw,
Slieve Croob

Slieve Croob, where the waters of the river Lagan first bubble up for air, takes its name – as those with even a smattering of Irish will tell you – from the words *Sliabh Crúibe*, words which are pronounced approximately as 'sleeoo krooba', and which translate, awkwardly but literally, as 'Mountain of the Hoof'. You might prefer Hoof Mountain, a name whose origins surely lie in the myriad mountainy mythologies of cattle, of bulls, of rustling and of wars.

To the conservationist, Croob, formed from igneous Caledonide rock, is part of the Mournes Area of Outstanding National Beauty, while Black Lough, shimmering darkly between the peaks of Dunmore and Dunturk on its eastern flank, is an Area of Special Scientific Interest, awash with scarce enough sedges, plus one of the Hypericums, Marsh St John's Wort, with Western Gorse, *Ulex gallii*, and the rare Irish damselfly, *Coenagrion lunulatum*, one of the many creatures grouped as *Béchuil* in Irish. The course of the Moneycarragh River, running south-east also from its Slieve Croob source, is, in autumn, a corridor of hazelnuts, *Corylus avellana*, while McCauley's Lake – east of the legendary site of the clan McCartan Castle at Magheratimpany

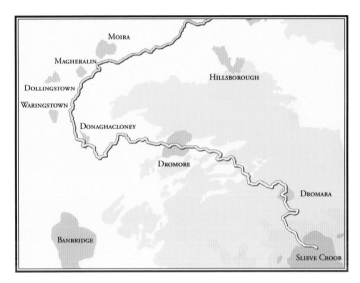

– hosts flocks of wintering and stately Mute and Whooper swan, *Cygnus olor* and *Cygnus cygnus*.

At Croob's summit, just west of the Lagan's source, where the townlands of Dree, Drinn, Dooglen, Slievenisky and Legananny all meet, at a calf-muscle-bracing 1,755 feet above the Irish Sea, there's a 90ft diameter cairn which has, over the centuries since it was first built in Neolithic times, been reorganised to form the Twelve Cairns which give this site its common name and which, even into the middle

GILLIAN LOTTON

of the as yet untroubled 1960s, attracted dancers and musicians on the first and second Sundays of August. 'Till then, for generations, children, through the warm afternoons, picked enough bilberries, *Vaccinium myrtillus* to the rector and schoolmaster – blaeberries to the locals, *Tom fraochán* to the priest – to fill the tinkers' pitcher. Later, after dusk, its was their elder siblings who leapt, legs akimbo, across the flickering flames of wood fires which burnt to embers by midnight, after when they might beget, if schoolmaster and priest had fallen into a *poitín* favoured sleep, another generation before rosey-fingered dawn crept in from the Irish Sea.

There are old boys from the townlands of Dree and Drin on the northern slopes; from Dunturk with its rath or Drumaroad with its church, primary school, post-office, raths and White Fort's souterain; from around the raths of Drumnaquoile, Ballywillwill, Backaderry and Ballymackilreiny south – or near the cashels of Cloghskelt west who'll tell you, winking, that there's something in Slieve Croob's waters, their assertion supported by the surprising number of world famous figures whose family roots are embedded in the area.

In 1761, Arthur Guinness, two years after he opened the St James' Gate Dublin brewery producing the world's favourite black stout, had his wedding cup engraved with the lion, the wild boar and Red Hand of Ulster, the armorial bearings of those Celtic aristocrats, the Magennises of Iveagh. And indeed Arthur's descendant, Edward Cecil Guinness, was elevated to the peerage in 1890 as none other than Baron Iveagh of Iveagh. But the less socially aspirational truth hidden in the Guinness Y-chromosomes, and so passed from father to son, was revealed in 2007 by geneticists at Dublin's prestigious Trinity College and confirmed a more humble origin within the family's DNA. As Patrick Guinness detailed in his own book *Arthur's Round*, his ancestors were peasants, not Gael aristos, and their origins can be traced to the McCartan – my mother's family – rather than the Magennis clan and in particular to a tiny hamlet or clachan, a cluster of farmsteads, at *Gion Ais*, which translates as 'wedge-shaped ridge' and which is now spelt as Guiness on Guiness Mountain on Croob's eastern slopes. The family name is thus not a patronymic, but a toponymic, derived from a place-name, not a family name.

But what else of the famous sons of the Lagan's source?

Well, when France's President, General Charles De Gaulle, a soldier who though no friend of England's Prime Minister Winston Churchill, had fiercely preserved his country's honour during World War II, came to Ireland on holiday in the summer of 1969, his thoughts turned to the tiny county Down townland of of Drumaroad, two miles south-east of Guinness, but still on the slopes of Slieve Croob, the source of the river Lagan. For it was from there that his Irish ances-

tors, John, the last McCartan chieftain, and his son Anthony, loosing Jacobites at the Battle of the Boyne, departed, as 'Wild Geese', Irish mercenaries in Frances armies.

The McCartans – and I'm one on my mother's side – who now spell their family name variously as MacArtan, Mc Cartan, McCartain or MacCarton, were chieftains of the Barony of Kinelarty and, further back – according to papers held in the Office of Arms in Dublin Castle – the direct descendants of the powerful Kings of *Eamain Macha*, a location remembered today in the name of the city of Armagh, home to Catholic and Protestant Archbishoprics of all Ireland.

The McCartans though prone to many financial political and misjudgments, plus romantically embellished memories, once held the county Down baronies of Kinelarty, Dufferin and parts of those of Castlereagh and Iveagh. But by 1600 much had been lost to the English and Scots colonists, with just a few strongholds remaining around the parishes of Ardinlea, Ballynahinch, Drumaroad, Drumnaquoile, Finnebrogue, Loughisland, Mageraknock and Mageratimpany. In 1605, during the reign of England's James I, Lord Edward Cromwell, governor of the Lecale, owner of Downpatrick and Dundrum's impregnable castle, drove a hard bargain, gaining many more McCartan lands while, in a one-sided exchange, making but a promise to bring up the 14 year old Patrick McCartan as a gentleman.

Whatever the merits of the agreement, Patrick was soon dead and his son (another Patrick) was helping take Newry in the bloody insurrection against the English Crown in 1641. Though he fought at the critical Battle of Benburb in 1645, the Irish clans were no match for Colonel Chichester's burnt-earth campaign which subsequently laid waste the family's land, much of which later became the property of the Forde family who still run an elegant house and estate at Seaforde.

Memories of these times left a bitter taste for years to come. For example in a later generation Rev. James O'Laverty, whose own mother was a McCartan, regarded any deal with the English, or the quitting for France, as such a betrayal that in his delineation of the family legacy he ignored the fascinating line of descent which extends from Anthony McCartan, born county Down 1680, who died in France 1753.

There was, in turn, Antoine McCartan (1716-1787); Andronicus Xavier McCartan (1764-1842); Marie Angelique McCartan who died in Lille as Madame Delannoy in 1852; Julia Marie Delannoy who died Madame Maillot in 1912. Jeanne Marie Maillot, born 1860, died as Madame De Gaulle in 1940, having given birth to Charles De Gaulle, who having been born on the 22nd November 1890, died 9th November 1970.

For De Gaulle's aide when he visited Ireland, Admiral François Flohic, a man much persuaded by tales of Ireland's romantic past, the McCartans were all heroes, the descendants of kings who had *'suffered despoilations throughout their history'*. Thus a number of this island's McCartans were invited to shake hands with France's tall saviour in the Drawing Room at *Aras an Uachtaráin*, Ireland's Presidential Residence, before the General sped off to lunch with the Taoiseach in Dublin Castle. Amongst the several so invited, but instructed not to stay for lunch, was the Rev. Fr. Denis McCartan and a nun, whose family name was O'Hare. There too, somewhat ironically were Mr and Mrs A. Forde, descendants of those who had gained McCartan lands following the Chichester suppression of Ireland's tribes.

Revealingly, Admiral Flohic's diaries of the visit had commented that: *'Given the continued British domination of Northern Ireland, there was no question of his (President De Gaulle's) being able to go there.'*

Several McCartans had written to the General, wishing to meet their hero. But it was the Admiral's embarrassingly reported interpretation of the situation which prompted other McCartans, including my own mother, an egalitarian by nature, to offer the riposte that if the war hero could not come north, she could not go south.

Which of us, whatever country we are in and whatever land we have come from, isn't, with the wind in our sails and a pint in our hand, the descendant of kings? But it seems that your humble author shares, amongst the skeins of blood lines, those not only of the Planter Hills of Hillsborough, but, on his mother's McCartan side, those of General De Gaulle and of the world's most famous brewer.

Meanwhile over Slieve Croob's cairn-scattered top, a buzzard, *Buteo buteo*, high in a vast sky and mewing 'pee-oo, pee-oo', scans the ground for lesser creatures. A meadow pipit, *Anthus pratensis*, perching on a withered stalk of Marsh thistle, *Cirsium palustre*, sings its trilling 'tsip', perhaps unwisely for their nests are the cuckoo's target nursery. Wheatears, *Oeanthe oenanthe*, distinguished by their white rumps and 'weet-chack' calls; plus grey wagtail, *Montacilla cinera*, and the white-breasted black dipper, *Cinculus cinculus*, call 'zit-zit' as they bob and flash by the rippling waters, further along the Lagan's course. Somewhere, distantly, a farmer's tractor changes gear. Close to the path, on the drain's edge, the star-shape of a tiny plant glistens. Back at the gate Chris Wilson's sculpture suggests the window of an abandoned homestead where a cross fashioned from rushes would have been hung, for good luck, on January 31st, St Brigid's Eve in the New Faith, goodness knows what in the older pagan times. Whin blossom dyed the hard-boiled eggs yellow for Easter. Bonfires were lit for good luck on May's Eve. July 12th is the Orange-

mans' Day, a day for Orange Lillies, August 15th is for the green, white and orange of the Hibernians.

Slieve Croob, a modest enough hill, reaching just 534 metres – or 1,755 feet if you prefer it – above sea level itself sits amongst a nest of lesser granite peaks, its lip a circle running clockwise from Ribadoo and Monahora at around 10 and 11 o'clock, past Guiness, Dunmore and Dunturk Mountains, Slievenisky, Slievenamoney, Slievehanny, Slievegarran, Beltraw, Slievenaboley, Deehommed and Cratlieve. This last, at 429 metres high, is where dolmen-fanciers will find one of their favourite 'Giant's Graves', Legananny, just two miles south-west of the Lagan's birthplace. Their other prize, another set of massive gravestones, is at the centre of the 'Giant's Ring' on the outskirts of Belfast, not far from the river's debouchment into the Irish Sea.

Fresh water feeds and waters the land and thus the creatures upon it. So the Lagan, even when it is little more than a stream running between county Down's drumlin hills, became home to peoples of the Neolithic Age, people whose civilisations left us, their successors perhaps, their stone monuments, many of them, loosely enough, called dolmens, the many varied Giant's Graves of previous generations. To the fanciful, the sheer dimensions of the constructions under which bones were oft times found, indicated not multiple burials strung out along a series of chambers, but the interment of a giant whose arms were perhaps flung outward and upward following the lines of what scientists now terms the 'horns' of the cairns embracing a forecourt.

Downstream from Dromara, in the townland of Lappogues – which takes its name, Little Bed, from the romance of Ireland's Romeo and Juliet, Diarmuid and Grainne – less than a mile north west of the weir by Bulls Brook there's what looks now like a loose scattering of Silurian boulders. But stand still. Look. There are stones lying about, running roughly 30 metres nor'-by-nor-west. Think. Then you'll just discern, by the field wall, six stones which give the suggestion of a semi-circular forecourt which would have led to what's still, just, recognisable as the outlines of what archaeologists deem a 'chambered long cairn' a four-chambered grave – another of these tumbled 'Giant's Graves'.

Further downstream, a mile and a half west of Dromore, and just south of the same road, the B2, and on the south bank of the Lagan, close under Nut Bank and Greenan Hill, there's a further cairn, this time a round one known locally as the Dumb Fort or the 'Pagan Grave'. Roughly 110ft by 80ft it is at times up to 8ft high despite the previous predations of farmers seeking building stones. Excavations in 1902 revealed a cist, a tunnel, 6ft long and 4ft 9 in at one end and 2ft 6 in at the other, roofed with two capstones. Inside were poorly preserved inhumed bones. There was another, smaller

cist nearby and previous editions of the OS map show a now invisible 'cromlech', another word for dolmen, 50 yards to the south-east. In the townland of Ballynaris, directly across the Lagan, today's maps also mark Phil's Fort lying between the B2 and the river, plus a further mound a mite further north-west. Indeed a close examination of Sheet 20 of the OSNI 1:50 000 Discoverer Series, without which no exploration of the Lagan's course can be complete, will reveal the little black stars which, with the accompanying words 'cashel' 'cairn' 'chambered grave' 'fort' or 'rath' printed beside them in little red letters, accompany the river's course from Croob to the sea. Those more dedicated, or indeed obsessed, will carry with them in the glove compartment on their explorations, a printout of the DOE/EHS scheduled monuments record which lists such sites, townland by townland.

But back to the river. From granite Croob, bubbling, widening, the Lagan's magical stream runs north, slipping under stone bridge after stone bridge at Finnis – whose village name comes from the Irish word *Fionnais* meaning White-Ridge – and Bell's to Dromara, *Droim mBearach*, Heifers' Ridge.

In tiny Finnis, with its bridge and its weir, there's still talk of the 'haunted' sycamore tree, whose demons were exorcised by a priest's acuity, opposite James King's public house by the Dree Hill bridge and its most curious weir. There's also chat about the 94ft long souterrain, 6ft by 5ft wide, its ceiling

Stories in Stone,
Legananny Dolmen

DREE HILL

DREE T.D

GILLIAN LITTON

granite slabs, in this, the Lagan's first village. This 9th century tunnel, a hiding place for stores and people in times of strife, sits in a field off the Carrigagh Road 2½ miles south of the village crossroads. Named Binder's Cove and first gated off by a mid-19th century rector, its is now – courtesy of the farmer and thanks to Banbridge's District Council – open to the public over the summers, with its sometimes claustrophobic gloom softly illuminated by solar-generated light. In winter a key may be borrowed from O'Hare's Garage. The Catholic Church of St. Michael the Archangel, designed in 1833 on the site of a 16th century predecessor by architect Thomas Duff, was rebuilt in 1887. Genealogists report that previously its parishioners were buried next their Protestant neighbours in the graveyard of the handsome St John's Church of Ireland in Dromara, the next settlement on the Lagan's course. That church too was constructed in the early 19th century on the site of a Catholic predecessor burnt in the insurrection of 1641 and finally destroyed in 1690, the year of Protestant King William III's victory of Catholic James at the Battle of the Boyne.

Dromara, once called Annesborough, and on the very lower slopes of Croob, was settled on land given to Rorye Magennis by Elizabeth I but forfeited to my own ancestors on my father's side, the Hills of Hillsborough, after the bloody massacres of 1641. It owes its past prosperity to both the Lagan's water-power and to its capture by James Black, the

Red Gate and River,
Dromara Bridge

man who founded the Dromara Flaxworks complete with linen bleachworks, rettery and beetling mill on its banks. The town's much-renovated Church of Ireland Church, with its solid three stage tower topped with four pedestals, replaced an abandoned predecessor.

The First Dromara Presbyterian Church stands at Ardnatrannagh. A spare meeting house in style, it is also a replacement, having been built in the 1826 over its early 18th century thatched predecessor, a place whose worshippers had previously met, since the year 1711, in John Baxter's Stackyard. Rectangular, seven windows wide and with three entrances, it bears an inscription over its central door urging those who read it to:

'Remember the Sabbath Day
To Keep it Holy'

In its graveyard is a stone bearing the words:

Here is interred The Revd James Birch, Presbyterian Minister of
the Parish of Dromara
Reader! If exemplary discharge of his important duties
For 56 years
If a candid liberal Christian Spirit,
If the warmest affections towards his fellow men,
Excite an interest;

His memory will live in your breast,
Then death shall have erased the impressions
So fondly cherished and deeply engaged
Upon the hearts of his Flock.
Obit October 29th 1820, aged 80.

A court house, a market house, plus a Second Presbyterian and a small Methodist Chapel, completed the town's original public appurtenances. Dromara's two storey, three bay, Glebe House, now in private hands, just west of St John's Church where the Banbridge and Dromore Roads meet, was built in 1821 to designs by one of Lord Downshire's two favourite local architects, either James McBlain or Charles Lilley. It is an L-shaped two-storey and basement, former and typical, Church of Ireland rectory, owned previously by the Rev. Hannington Elija Boyd, the cleric who sealed Finnis's 'cave'. The Glebe's peculiar enhancement is a 'black hole' in its basement, all the better for 'its squarson to consign', as the incomparable architectural historian Charles Brett put it 'offenders'. On the town's Hillsborough Road, at Mullaghadrin, stands the charming former manse, built to a one-and-a-half-storey pattern much beloved by Victorian Presbyterians.

The cathedral at Dromore, like most matters episcopalian in Ireland, is said to trace its roots back to St Patrick who decided where all holy places should be built. It is written that he had a vision, perhaps in Downpatrick, of a host of

Dromore Cathedral

angels hovering over a valley in the distance outside the east window of where he was celebrating mass. Declaring that a monastery be founded on that very spot over which the angels soared, his wishes had to wait two centuries till *St Mo-Cholmóg*, aka St Colmán, titular saint of churches in both Scotland and Wales and whose feast-day is June 7th, fulfilled them. Indeed successive cathedrals at Dromore were dedicated to St Colmán till the name was changed to that of Christ the Redeemer by Letters Patent of James I in 1609.

Rich by the 12th century, the monastery was much raided by the Vikings but then faded into insignificance with little being known about it through the 13th and 14th centuries except that it was so poor it was considered sufficient punishment to banish to Dromore two knights, Sir J. Holt and Sir R. Belknap who had been convicted of treason against Richard II, and by the 15th century Henry VII was advised that 'none would remain upon the bishopric'. Thus succeeding bishops, about whom much confusion reigns, resided, absentees, in England before the arrival first of the Frenchman, Yvo Guillen, and then the Greek, Georgius Braua, both of whom ignored the opposing claims on Dromore by the 15th century absentee Bishop Egeremond.

James I restored its fortunes in 1609, gifting it lands and thus enabling Bishop Jeremy Taylor to rebuild what ruins there were left there by 1662, all previous efforts having been tossed

in the fighting of 1641. Indeed so great was the destruction wrought at that time that only a much weathered, much reconstructed – with a mainly modern shaft – 9th century ring-headed Cross with 6ft wide arms, removed from the market place, plus a 17in by 12in stone called 'St Colmán's Pillow' in the south wall of the chancel, obviously recall earlier days. However a 1613 Bible, inscribed 'The Gift of John Straker' is encased in the nave, having been recovered after being stolen in 1614.

Jeremy Taylor, a barber's son who grew up in a pub, 'The Wrestlers' Inn', Cambridge, and who was imprisoned as a supporter of Charles I on the instructions of the Lord Protector Cromwell. After the English Civil War he became Bishop of Down and Dromore in the reign of Charles II. Portrayed in sculpture on one of the eight charming wooden misericorae, ledges on which to rest during prayers, in the town's plain neat Anglican Protestant Cathedral of Christ the Redeemer, he was known as the 'Shakespeare of Divines' and, as such, much admired for his prose style by Samuel Taylor Coleridge, William Hazlitt and Thomas de Quincey. He was particularly praised for his authorship of *Holy Living* and *Holy Dying*, best-selling, and somewhat garrulously sonorous, tomes of 'rules' for Anglicans who found themselves without a priest under Cromwell's Republic. He wrote : 'As our life is very short, so it is very miserable; and therefore it is well that it is short'. His ancestor, Dr Rowland Taylor had, after all,

*Bishops Bridge,
Dromore*

been burnt at the stake by Roman Catholic Queen Mary and Jeremy's theological tussles with county Down Presbyterians had made his bishopric 'a place of torment'. He died, aged fifty-four, in his house in Castle Street Lisburn, before a pet project of his, a barn church, built with bulls' eye glass windows at Upper Ballinderry, could be consecrated.

Bishop Thomas Percy (1729-1811), who took down – and then rebuilt – the cathedral's tower in 1808 and added its Percy Aisle, plus a slate roof to replace the previous oak, was a tobacconist's son. He edited the *Reliques of Ancient English Poetry*, an early collection of popular English ballads which was still in print, in a facsimile edition, in 1996. It was a book greatly admired by William Blake, Oliver Goldsmith, Samuel Taylor Coleridge, John Keats, Dante Gabriel Rosettii and William Wordsworth. Citing Miguel Cervantes' *Don Quixote* as his favourite book, Thomas, a polymath linguist fond of shooting, horse racing, cards and pleasure gardens, died in the Bishop's residence in Dromore on the 30th September 1811. Indeed both Bishops, Taylor and Percy, are buried within the Cathedral, as is Percy's wife, a woman referred to as beautiful 'O Nancy' in one of the bishop's poems, a verse claimed by Scotland's genius Robbie Burns as: "the most beautiful ballad in the English language".

Admiringly, in Percy's funeral sermon, his successor George Rust described his predecessor as having : "the good humour of a gentleman, the eloquence of an orator, the fancy of a poet, the acuteness of a schoolman, the profoundness of a philosopher, the wisdom of a chancellor, the sagacity of a prophet, the reason of an angel and the piety of a saint".

Favoured neither by Catholics nor Presbyterians, Percy's apse was criticised as a too 'French' addition and the double church appearance of nave and north aisle, divided by seven low pointed arches, may bewilder the newcomer.

The Bishop's Palace has been demolished, but Bishop Taylor's pithy poems aside, the town has much more to recommend it: the old viaduct of the Banbridge to Lisburn railway; two stone bridges over the Lagan, the Downshire and the Regency, conserved by their B1 Listing. Listed to a similar grade are a number of houses in both Bridge Street and Meeting Street, as are its Cowan Henderson Hospital, the Ulster Bank and the Town Hall. Gallows Street's name raises an eyebrow, as do the preserved stocks in the town's centre.

Towards the north-eastern boundary of the town, south of the Mound Road, stand the remains of town's 40ft high by 65ft across 'Great Fort' or 'folkmote', an Anglo-Norman feudal motte or raised earth mound, beside a 100ft wide southern defensible bailey, all overlooking a curve of the Lagan at the edge of the colonist's influence at the beginning of the 13th century. Excavations, in 1951, recorded evidence of a

*Winter Walkways,
Dromore Viaduct*

timber palisade, plus the shards of a 13th century glazed jug. More recognisable will be Dromore Castle, a 17th century square three-storey stone tower of the type described in detail in my book *Lecale - St Patrick's County Down*. Roughly 30ft square, with a square projection to the east, it overlooks the Cathedral and was built, it is presumed, by William Worsley for the protection of his brother-in-law John Tod, Bishop of Dromore. Defensive slits, open and re-closed, survive on every floor. Off the Banbridge Road and surrounded by more modern buildings, and notably ruinous, its re-stabilisation re-began in 2007.

Lagan Lodge, Listed B1, is a truly delightful six bedroom hip-roofed Georgian house, once complete with weavers' pay-office and its yard's lapping room, Clanmurry, built for Thomas McMurry soon after he came to Dromore from Waringstown whilst pioneering cambric handkerchief manufacturing for the fashion houses of London and Paris. On the Lower Quilly Road to the village's west, is a solid, well-proportioned B1 Listed Georgian house built for William Mc-Clelland son-in-law of the linen innovator Thomas McMurry of Thos McMurry & Co. It later passed through other linen barons' hands, the Jardines, the Sprotts and the Baxters. Further B1 Listings have been designated to Carnew Cottage, Marybrook, Ashfield and Ballyvalley House

Writing of Donaghcloney in 1837 the gazetteer Samuel Lewis commented 'There is scarcely a house in the parish that is not, in some way connected with this manufacture of linens, lawns, cambrics, diapers, sheetings and other articles.' He was writing of an industry which had begun during the reign of Queen Anne and been developed by Samuel Waring who brought Quaker craftspeople from the north of England. He himself built, with his own hands, his own first spinning wheels and it was his ancestor William who had built Waringstown House, in what became known as Waringstown to the north, in 1667. A bell, which was dragged from the Lagan mud and which now hangs in the tower of Waringstown's CoI church, bears a crudely fashioned inscription, which reads 'I belong to Donagacloney'. The village's name, in Irish, was *Domhnach Cluana*, the 'Meadow Church', a medieval Catholic establishment remembered now for its Laganside graveyard beside Donaghcloney Bridge. Catholics however worship in Tullylish, a parish with two further Catholic chapels, a Quaker Meeting House, plus one for Free Presbyterians, and four for other Presbyterians, while there are three CoI places of worship.

But it was the comparative liberalism of the 1890s which prompted the Liddells, owners of the village's linen mill, one still working on Main Street in 2002, to build the neat workers' houses in William Street which, with other similar buildings, gardens and allotments were acquired for improvement

Winter Weir,
Donaghcloney Weir

by the Donaghcloney Housing Association in 1997. The village's linen business was begun by David Dempster in 1708 for a lease which included 'one couple of two fat hens', a fee no doubt honoured by his descendant, the linen draper Marmaduke Dempster. Consisting of bleachworks, beetling mills, wash-house and drying loft, all water-powered, it passed through the hands of the Browns and the Nicholsons of Banoge till becoming the power-loom damask premises of Messers William Liddell & Sons in 1871. Its octagonal red-painted brick chimney, the village's pride, rose to 145 feet.

By contrast, Scottish sandstone Straw Hill, a B1 Listed house on the village's Hall Road, probably designed by the splendid Scotch architect William Playfair whose signature is also on Lurgan's Brownlow House, was built for William Nicholson, a merchant who had benefited from the boom in linen manufacture. Succeeding a modest farmhouse, Nicholson's pretensions had him name it Donaghcloney Hall before reverting, sensibly, to the original name.

Donaghcloney's Church of Ireland had been built where, tradition goes, St Patrick had outlined its foundations on the ground with his pastoral staff. But during the 1641 insurrection the congregation and clergy moved to the security of Waringstown leaving behind no trace of the original. A village school, built in 1903, was closed in 1970 to become St Patrick's Church of Ireland in Donaghcloney.

Neighbouring Waringstown's Holy Trinity Church of Ireland, complete with its gothic windows, tower, steeple and bells, plus the later addition of north transept and southern aisle, is of a rather neat appearance though it is of an intriguing meld of Jacobethan and Victorian styles. Now Listed as B+ for its architectural importance by the Environmental and Heritage Service, it was begun in 1681 after William Waring had obtained an Act of Parliament to move its position from the site of the old Parish Church at Donaghcloney Bridge and thus to encourage Protestants to settle there. The oak carvings on the pulpit are by the hand of the Rev. Holt Waring, dean of Dromore who, in his younger days, was Commanding Officer of the 3rd Iveagh Yeomanry, Chaplain of the Royal Down Militia. The oak roof is much talked of.

Waringstown's formal Italiante-style Presbyterian Church, also Listed B+, with campaniles to its front corners and standing to the north-east in the townland of Tullyheron, dates from 1853. Its design is, somewhat improbably, attributed to Sir Charles Lanyon. Donaghcloney's roughcast Presbyterian Church, formally known as Ballynabragget Seceding, dates from over a century earlier in 1750.

William Waring himself had bought the lands from Cromwell's dragoons and built his fine mansion, a elegant house from which he was driven by the forces of the Irish till it was recaptured by William III's Duke of Schomberg who bedded himself there for two nights on his way to the Battle of the Boyne. William Waring, who had escaped to the Isle of Man, was then outlawed by James II. So it was left to Samuel, who having learnt the linen business in Holland and Belgium, brought his enterprise and expertise back to the family estates.

Fine houses, including of course Waringstown House, decorate the Laganside acres. Annaghanoon House, at the end of a long lane in the townland of the same name, on the Banbridge Road, is elegantly Georgian and Listed, with its two storeys and its five bays. Tradition claims it once had three storeys. Two houses on the Clare Road, No. 150 plus another at No. 163 called Diaper Hill, its name taken from the linen trade, are both Listed B1s. Cambray House, B1 Listed, to the north, was designed by Sir Charles Lanyon in 1840 for John Henning who took over McMurray's fine cambric manufactury and who went on to win the UK's sole Gold Medal for cambric in the Great Exhibition of 1851. Indeed even the town's War Memorial benefits from the same degree of Listing.

The vernacular 17th century farmhouse at Edenballycoghill, otherwise 98 Dromore Road, is a B1 Listed yeoman planter's house, wonderfully restored in 1999. Less modest, though built around the same time, Waringstown's The Grange, also B1 Listed on Main Street, was presumably built for William

Waring before he graduated to Waringstown House itself. Originally a single storey cruck house, it is thought to have been enlarged for a weaver brought in from what used to be termed the Low Countries of the Netherlands and Belgium. Left empty in the 1970s it was, under public pressure, claimed by the Craigavon Development Commission who sold it to the indefatigable buildings conservationist John Lewis Crosby who then restored it to its former black-stone glory with its seven bays of windows. Lamb's Island a Regency farmer's villa beside Moylan's Fort on the Banbridge Road was once occupied by the Presbyterian cleric, the Rev. John Sherrard whose 'usefulness' was 'thought to be over' by his Tullylish congregation when he reached the age of 83. Nine years later the History of Congregations, perhaps in consequence, described him as 'a peppery old gentleman'.

The Plantation brought to Ulster the particularly English oak butt-purlin roof construction of the very grand Waringstown House, one of the finest in the province and certainly one of the first to be built without defensive parapets, though it occupies the site of a previous defensive fort. It has instead Dutch and Scottish gables. Designed by James Robb, one of Inigo Jones's assistants, it is set back from the Banbridge Road in the townland of Magherana and, dating from 1667, it was built on land bought from Cromwell's dragoons by William Waring. King William's man, the Duke of Schomberg commissioned its bake-house on his route to the Battle of the Boyne after he dismissed James II's troops from the mansion. The owner, in 2002, who had done much to restore time's predations, was a descendant of the original William Waring, a man whose brother Thomas, a tanner of Belfast's Waring Street, had a son who became Jonathan Swift's friend at Trinity College Dublin. Swift later proposed to, and was refused by, Jane Waring, his friend's sister, a woman he preferred to call 'Varina'. The real Jane is presumed to have lived in the Waring household at what was No. 30 Waring Street, a thoroughfare running down to the salt-pans on the Lagan's left bank.

Further downstream Magheralin's, or "Maralin's" as it is locally pronounced, pride lies, for some, not just in its most excellent surviving planters' houses, namely Blacklion and Drumcro, down by the New Bridge over the river Lagan, but principally in its Church of the Holy Trinity. For the church's stained glass windows, by Lady Glenavy, by A.E. Child and by Michael Healey, depict a number of Ulster's own saints, Columba and his oak, Comgall with his beard, Patrick despatching a snake, Gall throwing idols into Lake Constance.

St Patrick, the legend goes, travelled the Lagan by boat on his missions, mentioning Magheralin. But the first records of a monastery there are of 7th century Ronan Finn's, situated where a small tributary enters the main river at Feney, now across the main river. Despoiled by John de Courcy's Anglo-

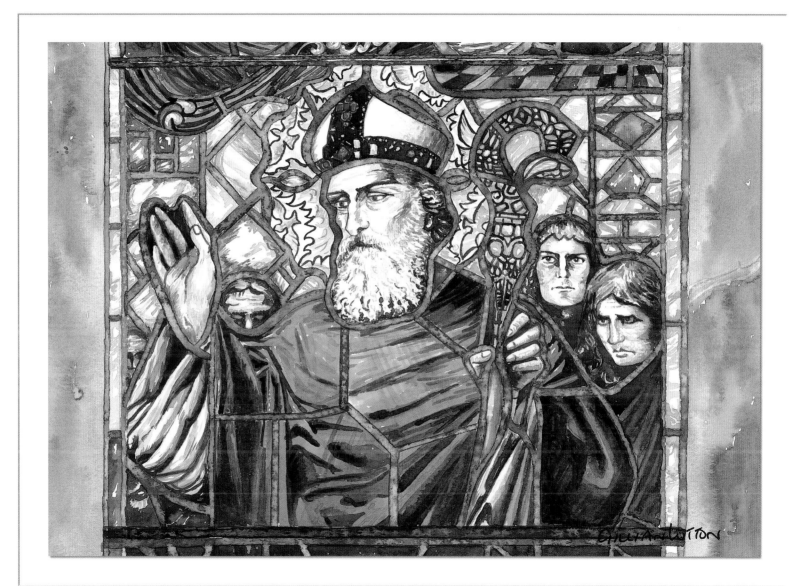

A Picture in Glass,
Church of the Holy
Trinity, Magheralin

Normans and restored as a pro-Cathedral in the 17th century, the monastery's Ronan's bell, Clough Rua, the Red Stone, was hidden in many places including Moira Castle before being restored to the Church of St Patrick in 1843. It is now held in Scotland's National Museum of Antiquities, while St Patrick's church graveyard still displays the remains of 15th and 16th century buildings.

Early military maps show the town of Magheralin's importance, recording it long before either Donaghacloney or Dromore. The settlement's heroes include St Colman who banished the settlement's disturbing demon, plus John Macoun, born 1813, a naturalist who explored the Canadian Rockies and wrote *Flora and Fauna of Canada*. The society painter Sir John Lavery, whose American wife conducted simultaneous and quite brazenly public sexual affairs with Britain's Prime Minister David Lloyd George and Ireland's revolutionary hero Michael Collins, attended the school beside the Catholic church.

There are excellent brown trout, *Salmo trutta fario*, with their lovely spots, to be caught on the fly – and on spinner and worm if you must in high summer downstream between Steps and Spencer's bridges – from March to September. The Iveagh Angling Club's permission is needed for the seven miles of river downstream of Dromore, under Thornyford Bridge, over Maggy's Steps, past Donagacloney, under Edenballycog-

ghill's Geehan's Bridge, then the Forge and Steps Bridges to Newmill and Spencer's Bridges. Upstream, between Dromore and Dromara, at the weir at Lappogues, and even up to Slieve Croob, you'll see brown trout and downstream, from Spencer's to Halftown Bridge, there are some trout. But from there to Lisburn there are many pike. Spinners use Devons, while the Medium Olive with Butcher on the tail will suit the wet-flyer. After a spate, try a Peter Ross on the tail. Grey or Red Quills are often the chosen dry flies.

Away further down the Lagan, the best coarse fishing is to be had between the Stranmillis Weir and Shaw's Bridge. There, there's a fine chance for slow moving Bream, *Albramis brama*; Gudgeon, *Gobio gobio*; carnivorous Pike, *Essox lucius*; the red-irised Roach, *Rutilus rutilus*; the slippery Eel, *Anguilla anguilla*, and the golden-irised Rudd, *Scardinius erythrophthalmus* plus that most beautifully marked of all Ireland's freshwater fish, the Perch, *Perca fluviatilis*, dark striped and red-finned in all its glory. A mite upstream, off a tributary, there are farmed Rainbow Trout in Hillsborough's Forest Lake and brownies in the Ravarnet, while downstream Grey Mullet, *Mugil chelo*, rise to the surface temptingly and some say they've seen a Salmon, *Salmo salar*.

However, there's hardly a public bar-room balladeer in the province of Ulster who doesn't know of the town of Magheralin for an entirely different reason: *The Ducks* (though some

Morning Mists,
Magheralin Bridge

sing this as 'The Docks') of *Magheralin*, one of whose many versions runs:

> Oh it's just a year ago today I went to see the Queen
> She dressed me up in satin and its colour it was green
> She decked me out in medals and they were all made of tin
> 'Ah go home' sez she 'ye boy-ye, ye'r' the mayor of Magheralin'.

Chorus: *Oh it is the finest city in the real old fashion style*
> A credit to the County Down, the pride of the Emerald Isle
> It has the finest harbour for the bread carts to sail in
> And if ye' ever sail to Ireland you'll sail by Magheralin

> Oh you've all heard of Napoleon, Napoleon Bonaparte
> He conquered half of Europe but left the other part
> He tired to conquer Ireland but they would not give in
> And he died in St. Helena when he thought of Magheralin

Chorus

> Oh you've heard of Cleopatra the treasure of the Nile
> And how she conquered 'Tony with one alluring smile
> She tired to conquer Ireland but they would not give in
> And they bate her out with cabbage leaves in the town of
>   Magheralin

Chorus

> Oh you've heard of good King William, King William crossed the Boyne
> With a hundred thousand balls of wax and a thousand balls of twine
> And then he gave the orders for the cobblers to begin
> For to make a hundred pairs of boots for the ducks of Magheralin

Chorus

> Oh you've heard of Mussolini that great Italian bum
> And how his troops in Africa were always on the run
> You've heard of Winston Churchill he always wore a grin
> For he knew the Ulster rifles were all born in Magheralin

Chorus

Though Moira traces its history back to Tara's king beating Comgall, Ulster's royal, in a battle of AD 637 near Pretty Mary's Fort, a battle remembered in Sir Samuel Ferguson's epic poem, *Comgall*, pretty Moira was, de facto, created in the 18th century by Sir Arthur Rawdon. He laid out its attractive broad main street of black-stone houses with carriage archways and elegant fanlights. Little but the foundations of Rawdon's Castle remains, but ornamental ponds and a wide grassy avenue leads into the demesne from St John's AD 1725 parish church whose doors were taken from the Castle's ballroom. Inside St John's a window commemorates the Logans, one of whom, James, botanist and major contributor to Benjamin Franklin's Library Company of Philadelphia, became that

Gateway to a Fort,
Pretty Mary's Fort

city's right-wing mayor. Methodism's founder John Wesley preached here in 1760 and, in 1835, William Butler Yeats, grandfather of the painter Jack Yeats and poet W.B. Yeats, became the church's curate. Hume Highway, between the Australian cities of Sydney and Melbourne, is named for Rev. James Hume, father of one of the most famous Antipodean explorers, Hamilton Hume. James's memorial rests in the town's Unitarian graveyard.

Berwick Hall, two storeys of thatched yeoman's cottage dating from 1700, stands south-east of the village. Crew Mount, well to the north, but still within this book's brief, at Glenavy, is a well constructed three-bay, two-storey Georgian farmhouse near, as its name suggests, Crew Hill's ancient boulder, revered by some as the site of 'The Spreading Tree of the Hill', crowning place, according to the Annals of the Four Masters, of the antique Kings of Ulidia or Ulster. Restored Ballance House in the townland of Ballypitmave, off the road to Glenavy, which itself is a pretty village with a three-arched bridge beside St Aidan's church, commemorates the birth here, in 1839, of John Ballance, social-reformist Prime Minister of New Zealand from 1891-93. But more famous locally perhaps was Francis Rawdon, 2nd earl of Moira and later Marquis of Hastings, who fought for the British, during the struggle for American Independence, at the Battle of Bunker Hill. But this book's author favours several other Moirianians: the Moravian Basil Patras Zula; Elizabeth Rawdon, 3rd wife

to the 4th baronet Sir John Rawdon; linguist Anne Lutton and her cousin William Lutton, surely relations by marriage to the creator of this volumne's painterly illustrations.

Anne Lutton's memoir, *Memories of a Consecrated Life* (1791 – 1881), recalls the coming of Methodism to Moira whilst her one volume of 1,000 verses sets out its virtues in its title, *Poems on Moral and Religious Subjects*. Whilst her books' titles may seem to promise the forbidding and the fustian, this thirteenth child of a long marriage recalls tales of the ghost of the Countess of Moira, of how Oliver Cromwell's men had blown up the chapel by the Lutton family burial ground at Old Seagoe, plus how the Reverend Thomas Waring went to his eventual death still proud that he had, in 1756, defied the Earl of Moira's request to allow the Methodist preacher John Wesley to preach in his parish church. Anne, by now a fervent Methodist preacher herself, and credited almost improbably with being fluent in over fifty languages including Arabic, Chaldeian, Ethiopian, French, Greek, Irish, Russian, Samarian, Spanish and Syrian, was also a close friend of the Langtrys of Kilmore, a family whose relations included the husband of Lily Langtry, King Edward VII's most celebrated mistress.

Anne's memorial, in Old Seagoe Parish Church, lies close to that of her cousin William Lutton who had toyed with the idea of a medical career in Paris but abandoned it on a matter

Under the Thatch,
Berwick Hall, Moira

GILLIAN LUTTON

of conscience returning to Breagh as a land surveyor working in the main for Lord Lurgan and the Great Northern Railway. While it is to be presumed that he spoke French, his principal diversion was to compile a dictionary of the local dialect, 'Montaighisms' (pronounced Munchies) words and sayings gathered in the boggy parish of Montaigh which was later edited by the antiquarian Francis Joseph Biggar, thus differentiating between a 'skelp', a slap of the hand to the head, and 'smolloch' which is a cuff to the head with the knuckles. Many such words will still be found in use but William's bowdlerised text gave rise to much broader humour in a number of risqué Limericks, including one which begins:

> *"There was an oul' wan from the Munchies*
> *Whose language would surely affront y'ees"* .

Elizabeth, Baroness Botreaux, Hungerford, Moylens, Hastings of Hastings and Hastings of Hungerford – and countess of Moira – married her husband purely out of boredom for he was, according to gossip, 'something of a poltroon'. An intellectual, a wit and a bluestocking, she defended the early feminist author Mary Wollstonecraft against attacks from the clergy, debated literature with Bishop Thomas Percy at Dromore and became the models for 'Mrs Hungerford', 'Lady Oranmore' and the 'countess of Annaly' in the wonderfully satirical novels of Maria Edgeworth. Politically, she supported Armagh and Down's agrarian movement, the Hearts of Steel,

and protested to Lord Castlereagh against the army's brutal suppression of the United Irishmen. But linen was never far from anyone's thoughts in the Lagan valley and so she hosted a fancy-dress ball raising money in its workers favour.

Industrial archaeologists have mapped the Lagan's contributions to the economy back to the early 19th century, detailing the locations of beetling mills and bleachworks, cornmills and scutchmills from Dromara's Woodford downstream to Dromore and thus onwards along the river's course. Past Donaghacloney, Waringstown, Dollingstown, Magheralin and Lisburn to Belfast, the Lagan's power added to the mix the sawmills, weaving factories, hem-stitcheries and Cambric works, plus a distillery at Culcavy, a brewery at Waringstown. Waterpower, driving geared wheels and later turbines, was always the driving force. Long abandoned to first coal-fired steam engines and then electricity, the 21st century's recognition of the dangers of reliance on fossil fuels, the Lagan's flow, like the wind which drove the windmills' sails, an elemental 'green' force, is slowly being rediscovered.

The bleachworks of the 18th century needed clean water to soak the linen cloth in a *'keeve'* before it was put out to grass on the green, then repeatedly *'bucked'* or boiled with wood-ash *'lye'* and *'bran'* and steeped in buttermilk till it was sufficiently whitened.

A Sleepy Sunday,
Moira Main Street

GILLIAN LUTTON

But linen's history has longer roots, for, back even in the 15th century Lagan yarn fed the looms of northern England till the Plantation brought English weavers to Ulster long before Louis Crommelin and his fellow French Huguenots settled around Lisburn conscious of a traditional workforce well versed in the trades.

Flax, *linum usitatissimum* to a botanist, from which linen, that most elegant of all cloths is wrought, was known to the Egyptians, the Greeks and the Romans before it spread west in the Middle Ages, its poignant blue flowers atop the two-to-four foot high stems promising a further beauty to come, with a crop sown in March, ready to be laboriously pulled by hand in August. Then tied in *'beets'*, it was *'stooked'* to dry while the seeds ripened before they were *'ripped'* or *'combed off'* to be sown for next year's crop.

But the flax plant has a woody core surrounded by a fibrous sheath and thus must be decomposed by *'retting'* underwater in a soon to be foul smelling *'lint hole'*. This took up to two weeks before the plants were spread in the sun to dry. Next came pounding by hand, by flail, or *'scutching'* by machine, to separate the useless *'shows'*, the woody cores, from the stems against a wooden *'stock'*.

The flax was then combed or *'hackled'*, the resulting short fibres being called *'tow'*, the longer and more prized being deemed *'line'*. Tow was *'carded'* and spun for bedclothes and aprons. Line, being rolled up onto a vertical *'distaff'* by a *'spinster'* was then spun by a *'flyer'* with its hooks called *'hacks'* round a central *'spindle'*, becoming linen tread, wound onto a *'bobbin'*.

The yarn was then wound from bobbin to larger *'hanks'* each an astounding 3,600 yards long before being washed and bleached. Thus ready, it was wound again onto *'spools'* for the warp, and *'pirns'* for the weft. The warp forms the longitudinal threads running from the weaver's beam to the cloth beam. On a loom the weft are the cross threads, thrown by a shuttle across between the two separate layers of the warp, before a *'shedding'* device lifts and lowers the layers, answering to the weaver's foot-treadles.

At first, by the Lagan, as everywhere else, all these processes, from sowing the flax, to bleaching the cloth with wood-ash then *'calendering'* it or *'beetling'* it – a process which put a sheen on the cloth as it ran though a wooden box filled with stones – were worked by a farmer's extended family. Access to a horse powered *'gin'* which moved the beetling box backward and forward, hastened the work.

Louis Crommelin, who succinctly detailed many of these early processes, found them, he reckoned, primitively administered when he came to the Lagan valley thus he himself became, as it were, the gin, or the engine, of industrialisation.

The first water-powered scutching mill appeared in Belfast in 1740 when it was still being serviced from Lagan's hinterland. Then, in 1785, the White Linen Hall opened. By the 1914 boutbreak of World War I, after the Industrial Revolution, the city was known as 'Linenopolis' the largest linen centre in the world.

Shawled girls, on their way home from the mills, could be heard singing defiantly of one of their betters, the Doffing Mistress:

> *Oh, you'd easy know a doffer*
> *When she goes down the town*
> *With her long yellow hair*
> *And her ringlets hanging down.*
> *And her rubber tied before her,*
> *And her pickers in her hand,*
> *You'd easy know a doffer*
> *For she'll always get her man.*

But the Lagan wasn't always solely linen's. In 1778 Belfast's Charitable Committee put the Poor House childen to hand-spinning cotton. Thus the Poor House, two years later, had become the city's first cotton mill in an industry which, protected by tariff barriers from English competition, grew so rapidly that by 1825 3,500 workers were employed in enterprises such as Thomas Mulholland's in Winetavern Street, five storeys high, 70ft by 36ft boasting 5,364 spindles.

But the tariffs were lifted in 1824, the year of the patenting of the wet-spinning process for linen which made that industry more attractive to investors such as Mulholland who then turned from spinning cotton to spinning flax. By 1850 only four of Belfast's cotton mills had survived in a city of 29 flax spinning mills. Worse was to come for 'King Cotton'. At the outbreak of the American Civil War in 1861 the Northerner's Navy blockaded the Confederate ports, thus blocking all cotton exports. Cotton goods were no longer on the shelves: and had been replaced by goods from Ulster's new dynasties of 'Linen Barons' who saw increases of 100% in their annual profits. It could not last. With the revival of the British cotton industry after the end of the American Civil War, the spectre of insolvencies cast a dark shadow. Bankruptcies were common. Linen mills closed. But from Lisburn, along the lower reaches of the Lagan with its easy access to export markets through the bustling Belfast docks and quays, the enterprising survived, prospering even if their workers – who'd started in the mills aged eight and worked barefoot for miserable wages in dusty wet conditions which lead to bronchitis and tuberculosis – could be dead aged just 25.

Gillian Lutton

The Lady's Bridge,
Canal to Aghalee

Once the power which drove the mills of this island's premier linen valley, the river welcomes tributaries from Scallon Hill via Waringsford, from Skillyscolban through Blackskull, from the Aghalee Burn and the Goudy River, and from Hillsborough and Ravarnet. At Inisloughlin, east of Moira, in the townland of Balloonigan, downstream of the 18th century whinstone segmental-headed New Mill Bridge, before Spencer's Bridge down river, a canal aqueduct crossed the Lagan. This connected the Lagan lighters northwards under Broomhedge, Boyle's, Hertford and and Lady's Bridges, before they edged under the Railway Bridge and Hammond's at Soldierstown. Next they entered the Broad Water with its Hell Hole off Lurgansemanus, through Friar's Glen, past Aghalee before turning west decending into the valley of the Goudy River under the Sherrin's, Aghagallon, Goudy, Cranagh and Annaghdroghal Bridges to Ellis's Gut on Lough Neagh. The relics of the mill dam and mill of Aghagallon speak eloquently of a vanished past when Sir John Lavery the society painter, was born at Soldierstown south of Aghalee, a village recalled in the becoming ballad:

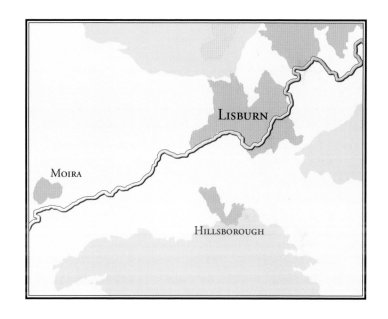

'Oh 'tis pretty to be in Ballinderry,
'Tis pretty to be in Aghalee;
But prettier far is little Ram's island
Sitting in under the ivy tree'.

The canal's northern locks, many still traceable, were the 18th at Aghalee, 19th Dan Horner's Wood Lock, 20th Sherrin's, 21st Bradley's, 22nd Cairn, 23rd Prospect, 24th Goudy's, 25th Fegan's Turtle Dove, 26th Cranagh Chapel and the final 27th at Ellis's Gut. South-east, the abandoned canal took a cross-country loop, now almost entirely buried under the M1 motorway, before rejoining the river at Union Locks at Sprucefield where it met its tributary, the Ravarenet River. For this was an essential element in a once improbably Grand Design to favour river-barge transport which would, under the power of horse, barge-pole, wind and engine, plod and puff slowly but ecologically soundly from Belfast to Lough Neagh on which converged a network of waterways which led all over Ireland:– via the Ulster Canal to Lough Erne and thence, by the Ballyconnell-Ballymore Canal to the Shannon to Limerick or Dublin on the Grand Canal; via the Lower Bann to Coleraine and the North Coast: via the Upper Bann and the Newry Canal to Newry; via the Coalisland canal to Ulsters coal mines at the town of the same name.

Indeed weekly coal lighters, making water from Coalisland across Lough Neagh to Portadown, Newry and Belfast were common enough by 1870, as was the transportation of great glass phials of sulphuric acid from Thomas Greg's and Waddell Cunningham's works on Lisburn's Vitriol Island. But inconsistent water levels on the Lagan Navigation were a problem, for there was a flight of four locks lifting the water level some 26ft from river to canal, all within a hundred yards of Sprucefield and ten locks, each 70ft by 16ft, descending to Lough Neagh. Besides, the coming of the railways, double-tracked from Belfast through Portadown and Newry to Dublin, single tracked from Antrim to Newcastle, sealed the canals commercial doom in a long-drawn out wake which still witnessed barges loaded with Lough Neagh sand-plying into the 1960s. Yet, making his first voyage, its principal funder the Marquess of Donegall, on board from Richard Owen's house at Moira right up to to Lough Neagh, on New Year's Day 1794, had had his dream fulfilled. Canal enthusiasts, in threnody, can still trace, map and memories to hand, the scant remains of past glories along the course of the disused canal, north, south and under the M1 motorway, from Broomhedge Bridge, by Exit 9 south of Derrydrummult, to Beechfield Bridge. From Lisburn, the Lagan Valley Regional Park's waterside towpath-walks make it a more rewarding task.

Just upstream of the New Bridge a little river joins the Lagan having passed on its way the fascinating Moravian church at Kilwarlin whose fame stretches, most curiously, back to the time of the Persian-Greek Wars of 480 B.C. That was when Xerxes's invading forces, 600,000 strong, were, according to the historian Herodotus, headed off at the pass by 300 Spartans and their allies led by Leonidas in the Battle of Thermopylae. "The Persian arrows will be so numerous that they will block out the sun", the Spartans were warned, prompting

Long Shadows,
Moravian Church
Kilwarlin Mora

Gillian Cotton

one warrior to murmur, in the stuff of legends: "Then we will fight in the shade".

For it's a story retold, topographically, in the Battle Garden in the grounds of Kilwarlin's little Moravain Church which stands just off the road in the townland of Corncreeny east of Hillsborough. The Moravians whose emblem is a lamb and flag surrounded by the Latin inscription: *Vicit agnus noster, eum sequamur* – which translates into English as: 'Our Lamb has conquered, let us follow him', – trace their beginnings back to AD 1415 and Roscecrucianism in Moravia, now part of the Czech Republic. Its religious practice was brought, in 1774, to the island of Ireland by John Cennick who established a congregation of some eighty souls on this spot in 1754, building its first church one year later. Almost a century on, its minister was removed to another Moravian church at Ballinderry and so both church, and its manse, fell into ruins though the remaining six elderly worshippers sought to preserve a vestige of a working schoolhouse.

Meanwhile, in Greece, in the 1790s, during another war of colonial resistance, this time against the Turkish empire, his father, a chieftain having died in that struggle, Basil Patras Zula, at the age of eleven years of age, became the head of his clan, thus gaining the extra accolade of a price on his head. Though he later saw action at the Battle of Missolonghi, Basil was so disgusted by the atrocities committed by both sides

during the 1820s Greek Wars of Liberation that he became a wanderer till taken up by a wealthy Englishman who directed him to Dublin where he was converted and ordained a minister of the Moravian church.

Arriving in Kilwarlin, Basil's energies and enterprise were seemingly boundless and so, on 13th October 1835 he had, at his own expense it is claimed, rebuilt the old stone church now neat, slated, roughcast and whitewashed with walls two feet thick. By 1836 forms could seat his congregation of 150 whose comforts included a small vestry and a gallery. While Basil, who died in 1844, lived in the rescued manse, his wife Ann ran a boarding school for 'Select Young Ladies'.

Basil would have known his Herodotus whose books have earned him the accolade of the world's first historian But he never forgot his homeland and so many of his energies were directed to moving the earth to recreate, in miniature, the landscape of the Battle of Thermopylae of 480 BC in the church grounds, an idea perhaps inspired by reading of the 16th century fashion for such 'Battle Gardens'.

Presumably Basil was also remembering another Spartan response. For when Xerxes pointed out the hopelessness of the Greeks' situation, outnumbered 200 to 1, and asked for the surrender of their arms, the Spartan leader Leonidas replied, with a brave obduracy which chimes well with Ulstermen past and present: 'Come and get them'.

The Battle of the Boyne in 1690, where the triumph of forces of Protestant William over Catholic King James, complete with the sieges of Enniskillen and of Londonderry can be justly said to have changed the course of European history. But just as importantly, a noisome five day 18th century diplomatic debate which took place in Hillsborough Castle, can be argued to have lead to independence of Britain's American colonies. For Benjamin Franklin, author of risqué essays, printer of pamphlets on equality, inventor of the Lightning Rod and the best-known scientist of his day, was the fledgling states' Ambassador at Large when he met with Wills Hill (1718-93) first Marquess of Downshire.

Wills was both my ancestor and a descendant of Moyses Hill who came to Ulster with the 1st Early of Essex in 1573 intent on colonising the counties Antrim and Down by 1607. The Magennis clan had held the area for centuries, basing their strength at Fox Fort near Crom ghlinn, Crumlin, the 'Crooked Glen'. They were challenged by the invading Anglo-Normans and then by first Sir Moyses Hill in 1611, and next by Moyses' son Peter who built a fort and a church which were in turn destroyed in the rebellion of 1641. However they were rebuilt by Peter's brother, Colonel Arthur Hill, in 1652 with the town emerging under Wills Hill from 1742 on-

wards. Endlessly ambitious, the Hills married for land, looks, money, power and titles. Thus Wills, before he met Franklin, had become Viscount Kilwarlin and earl of Hillsborough in the Irish peerage, plus having acquired the British titles of Baron of Harwich, Viscount Fairford and, again, earl of Hillsborough.

President of the Board of Trade and a fierce opponent of the Dublin Parliament, he became, by default, Secretary of State and a believer in colonial subjugation, a stand which led to Bostonians daubing the American houses of his supporters with 'Hillsborough paint' – a less than fragrant mix of faeces and urine. Not surprisingly Wills' meeting with Franklin, an attempt to solve the American independence question, did not go well and the resulting personal animosity fuelled the American War of Independence, thus gifting the village the ambiguously grand title 'The Birthplace of America'.

So, though he greatly improved Hillsborough, no historian has a good word to write about Wills and his legacy is summed up in the words of that gay political commentator and gothick horror novelist, Horace Walpole, 4th Earl of Orford, a diarist who observed was that Wills Hill was 'a pompous composition of ignorance and want of judgement', a view shared by 'Mad' King George III who wrote of him in 1776 'I do not know a man of less judgement than Lord Hillsborough'.

The parish church, St Malachy's, its foundations dating from 1662, is a more elegant and eloquent legacy to Wills and the rest of my family, the Hills. Begun by Peter and rebuilt and enlarged by Wills, then 1st Marquess of Downshire, as a replacement for the much earlier Chapel of Cromlyn in the grounds of Hillsborough Castle, it was dedicated to St Malachy and attached to the church at Drumbo during the papacy of Pope Nicholas in 1308. When an ancient willow was blown down in the storms of 1839, the Chapel's graveyard skeletons were revealed amongst its upturned roots.

The 'new' cruciform church, built of whinstone, cornered and buttressed with freestone, will hold 600 within its handsome pews and choir gallery. There is a peal of eight bells in the tower below the spare and elegant spire. Inside are two most splendid working organs, one by John Snetzler (1772) and the other by G. P. England (1795), plus an east window decorated to a design of cherubs by Sir Joshua Reynolds, plus a curious sculpture of a naked baby by Joseph Nollekens.

However Hillsborough itself is a most pretty village in the English style, its hilly Georgian main street dotted with gastro-pubs, antiquaries' emporiums, crafte shoppes and picturesque, picaresque art galleries including The Shambles, formally a cattle-pen, on the Dublin Road. The birthplace of Sir Hamilton Harty (1879-1941), the 'Irish Toscanini' as he became known when he conducted the Hallé Orchestra in the 1920s and who composed *Children of Lir*, is commemorated on Fairfort House with a blue plaque off the bottom of the hill. That's on Ballinahinch Street not far from where the elegant Church of Ireland's gothick revival St Malachy's Church was completed by Wills in 1772, up a long lime tree-lined avenue opposite a bold statue to the 4th Marquis of Downshire. A further memorial to Sir Hamilton, caved by sculptor Rosamund Praeger, lies close to the church.

Born Herbert Hamilton Harty, the fourth of ten children by Annie Elizabeth Richards and her husband, the church's organist, William Michael Harty, Hamilton was educated in the local school and by playing viola in the family's string quartet. No formal musical education ever followed, but, by 1894, aged fifteen, he had been appointed organist at Magheragall and a year later, to the same position at St Barnabas's, in Belfast. But this was a city whose lack of sophistication depressed him and so he moved to become organist at Christ Church in Bray where he found a mentor in the Royal Irish Academy's Professor of Music, a gifted and well-connected academic who furthered his skills as a sympathetic accompanist who would be chosen to play for Queen Victoria.

Hamilton's ambitions, social and musical, gained him the Organship of All Saints', Norfolk Square, London, a tenure which lasted but one week leaving him to make a living as a freelance accompanist, a perilous trade alleviated when he

St Malachy's Church,
Hillsborough

GILLIAN COTTON

married a Cheltenham gal, Agnes Helen Nichols, a principal with the British National Opera. Agnes' close friendship with an Hungarian conductor brought Hamilton his conducting opportunity with the London Symphony Orchestra, a position he soured by persisting in presenting his own works as a composer. Later he would replace Sir Thomas Beecham as the Manchester Hallé Orchestra's principal conductor, despite his reluctance to play modern composers and his insistent opposition to the appointment of female players to the band. Further disputes with the Hallé, which included a series of critically welcomed, but financially disastrous, London concerts, led to the parting of the ways and a new contract with the London Symphony Orchestra, an unhappy musical marriage which was soon unilaterally dissolved on account of the conductor's somewhat dictatorial management style.

Brought low by a malignant brain tumour which required the removal of his right eye, Hamilton composed *The Children of Lir*, premiered by the BBC Symphony Orchestra in 1939, a year before he put down his baton for the last time. Though knighted in 1925, and honoured by the establishment of an eponymous Chair of Music at Queen's University ten years after his death, the self-taught composer's musical legacy is mostly in abeyance outside his own province where the Ulster Orchestra is sure to perform his works on a regular basis. Estranged from his wife, and nursed by his secretary and 'intimate friend' Olive Elfreda Baguely, he died in Hove

with his ashes placed in Hillsborough's parish church where the Harty family's musical saga began.

Neither Sir Hamilton Harty's modest memorial, nor the 4th Marquis's bronze monument – dressed in his corduroys and wielding his blackthorn cane – close to it across Main Street, are any match for the 1873 statue of the 3rd Marquess atop a tall Doric column off the Dromore Road with, at its base, the family coat of arms and the inscription: *Per deum ferrum obtinuit*. The marquess had died, falling off his horse, in apoplexy. Wills, his ancestor, had hoped, vainly, that St Malachy's with its three-storey pinnacle and spire-topped tower plus its handsome interior, would become a Cathedral.

At the top of Hillsborough's hill is the Square with the Courthouse, begun in 1760 and which is now both Tourist Information Centre and a restored tourist Court where you might, had your ancestors been sheep stealers, imagine them being deported to Van Diemen's Land. Round the corner, beyond secure ornate wrought-iron gates, lie the rambling two storeys of Hillsborough House, dating from 1779 but much remodelled in the mid-19th century it was formerly Government House and the seat of Northern Ireland's Governors since 1924 till such fripperies terminated in 1973, another victim of the recent 'Troubles'. Still, on occasion, British Secretaries of State of varying abilities, have seen it as home and visiting Royals, including Prince Charles, still host garden parties in the extensive grounds. Guided tours are available for those not in receipt of either such Royal invitations or to the several charitable receptions held here each year.

Across the Square stands the impressive two-storey battlemented Gate House to Hillsborough Fort. It once commanded Kilwarlin Pass on the road from Carrickfergus to Dublin, the route travelled in 1690 by William, Prince of Orange, on his way to win the Battle of the Boyne. Cast-iron milestones in the Main Street give provenance, showing Dublin to be 70 (Irish) miles south. Begun on the site of a previous Magennes enclosure by Peter Hill in 1630 and completed by Colonel Arthur Hill twenty years later, this was deemed a Royal Fortress by Charles II and picturesquely Gothicked in the 18th century to become a delight for Hill family revels. Such public trysting as survives takes place in the adjoining public Forest Park complete with fishing lake and well shadowed paths.

Though the lake, fed from the Black Wood, is now purely ornamental, it feeds eventually into the Lagan tributary which flows north under first the Hillsborough Bypass, then through Culcavy and next under the M1 motorway which supplanted the Lagan Canal before passing Long Kesh's disused airfield home to the Ulster Aviation Society. This institution commemorates, amongst other matters, Dromore inventor Harry Ferguson making Ireland's first ever powered-

GILLIAN LUTTON

flight, in his self-built monoplane the Ferguson Flyer, from a snowy Hillsborough in 1909. North, past the Maze Race Course, the stream joins the Lagan between New Bridge and Young's Bridge where philosophers reflect on how Hillsborough a village, with nought but a freshwater to count on, boasts an annual Oyster Festival

The Maze itself leaves long memories. For thousands it is of quaffing champers and 'Black Velvets', a mix of Guinness and the 'bubbly' in the Down Royal Race Course's hospitality tents. Or of downing a quick pint in the bar, and then, having caught the flashing colours of your jockey's lucky silks across the almost flat and circular course, returned to your bookie, triumphant for a bunch of £5 notes as big as a cabbage – or, dismayed – your crumpled beaten docket to be discarded and left blowing in the wind.

For others it will always be The Long Kesh, later known as the Maze Prison, which held, in the main, the guilty paramilitaries, Protestant and Catholic, Loyalist and Republican, of Ulster's 'Troubles'. Much escaped from, and the site of the Republican hunger strikes, its future, as a memorial or as the place for the province's Sports Stadium, lies in the hands of the Assembly at Stormont.

Cities, even new ones such as Lisburn, become associated in the mind with certain individuals. Belfast, for instance, now

that it has an airport dedicated in his name at the mouth of the river Lagan, can be, to some people, as I discovered in Seoul, South Korea, footballer George Best's City.

For Lisburn you have a choice. Some would plump for Sir Fulke Conway, a Welsh Knight and brother to the 1st Lord Conway who might be said to have founded the place after James 1st granted him its lands in 1611. The walled gateway to Fulke's 1622 Killultagh Castle, in Castle Gardens, is all that survived the 'Great Fire' of 1707. A sandstone plaque commemorating the conflagration is now held in Lisburn's excellent Museum. Fulke's orders laid out Market Square, Castle Street, Bridge Street and Bow Street. Now their footprints are all that survives of his aspirational town grid for a place once called, in Irish, *Lios na gCearbhach*, Lisnagarvey, 'fort of the gamesters' which had been burnt to the ground previously in the rebellion of 1641, a massacre recalled in the name of Piper's Hill in memorial to a soldier musician whose head was blown off and rolled down its slopes in those bloody times.

A few might remember the names of the brothers Teeling, Bartholomew and Charles, United Irishmen born in Lisburn and arrested in September 1796. Bartholomew had sailed with General Humbert's French supporters of the insurrection, but was captured and hung after the Battle of Ballinamuck. Charles, though a supporter, took no physical part in

The Going's Good!
Down Royal Race
Course

51

the armed struggle, founding instead a linen-bleaching works in Dundalk and establishing and owning several newspapers including the *Belfast Northern Herald* and the *Ulster Magazine*, a journal which he edited from 1830-35. His various books and memoirs on the '98 were, as expected, not universally admired as they accused the Government of having scant regard for human rights. His eldest daughter, who'd edited his *Newry Examiner* from 1832 till 1840, married Thomas O'Hagan, later Lord Chancellor of Ireland.

Outside the Civic Centre, across the canal from Canal Street and near to midway between the gates of Hanna's Lock, there's a less than life-size seated statue remembering cardiologist Frank Pantridge complete with his lifesaving invention, the portable defibrillator. The Arts Centre's theatres, artists' studios, bar, bistro and art galleries are well complemented with – both on the island and on the Lagan's left and right banks, in the main between the weir below the Queen's Bridge and the pedestrian Millennium Bridge – an engaging series of public sculptures. A burnished steel 'Concentric Twist' marks the route of the Sustrans cycle path. Brian Connolly's witty bronze picture frame on his *Artist's Easle* comes fashioned with a stool. Ned Jackson Smyth's massive post-industrial bronze *Elements* of earth, fire an water offers resonances with the Lagan's linen trade. Bob Sloan's stainless steel *Tree of Dreams* proffers 5,000 fluttering copper leaves of memories. Karl Ciesluk's carved stone-relief fishes – eel, pike,

roach, stickleback and trout – all of them fish to be caught in the Lagan's waters, swimming beside the haunts of coot and moor hen.

The entrepreneurial will no doubt cite the names of linen barons such as William Barbour of Hilden while the more romantic fall, *n'est ce pas*, for Louis Crommelin (1652-1727), a Huguenot Protestant who, fleeing Louis XIV's religious persecution, was appointed by William III as Overseer of the Royal Linen Manufacture in Ireland. The Frenchman, who brought many with him whose particular family names survive in the region to this very day – and who did indeed have an improving influence on the quality of the cloth – is now, according to revisionist historians in the city's illuminating Irish Linen Centre attached to the Lisburn Museum, responsible for much less than that for which he was previously credited. To these authorities, the growth of the industry owes much more to the removal, in 1696, of the taxes on Irish linens when they entered England. However should Louis be your hero, you might commune with him while standing outside the site of the 18th century French Church, the Huguenot's place of worship till their numbers so diminished that they moved their obligations across Castle Street to the Anglican cathedral in whose graveyard they had already buried their dead. With its adjoining house, once Sir Richard Wallace's estate offices, the 'French Church' became, in turn, Lisburn Courthouse and later Lisburn's Town Hall, till the

Island Arts Centre

new Civic and Island Arts Centre was built on Vitriol Island in 2001.

In Magheragall, at 72 Ballinderry Road, Brookmount, stands austere and restrained Springfield, the two-storey white-painted stucco mid-Victorian designed by Thomas Jackson for Joseph Richardson, born 1821, Chairman of Railways and other companies, amongst them, the Co. Down Railway, the Northern Counties Railway (Lisburn's Railway Station, in Bachelor's Walk, was designed in 1890 by W. H. Mills for the Great Northern Railway), the Edenderry Spinning Co., The Island Spinning Co., etc, etc who lived there at the turn of the 19th century with his twelve children. With its canted bay window and hipped roof it is deemed the last of the linen magnates houses, unspoiled, to rest on the country Antrim slopes of the Lagan. Though its predecessor, an earlier Georgian Springfield, is much altered nearby, Springfield Mark II as it were, remained a Richardson possession till 1928, with its original owner remembered in the quaterain:

> *'Where'er the red gold floweth*
> *His coffers high to fill,*
> *His name is found, both sure and sound,*
> *At back of banker's bill.'*

On Orangemen's day, July 12th, some marchers will, outside Shannon's Jewellers, raise a toast William III, King Billy, who dined on that spot on his way to victory at the Battle of the Boyne along with the Duke of Schomberg, back in the days when it was the house of the Quaker goldsmith, George Benson

American Civil War buffs, and lovers of maritime art, should know of St Clair Augustine Mulholland, fifteenth child of Lisburn's Quay merchant and lighter-owner Henry Mulholland. Popularly assumed to have owed his forenames names, not to the day of his birth – April 1st 1839 – but as a tribute to his mother's, Henry's second wife Georgina Hester Agnes Sinclaire, reverence for St Augustine. St Clair, long after he emigrated to Philadelphia in the 1840s, became that city's respected Roman Catholic Chief of Police.

St Clair Augustine became a military man, fighting with the 116th Pennsylvanian Infantry's Irish Brigade in the American Civil War. Wounded in action at the Battles of Fredericksburg, Gettysburg, Wilderness, Mattaponi and Totopotomy he was brevetted Major-General in 1864 having been voted the Congressional Medal of Honour at Chancellorsville.

Serving as US Pension Agent under Presidents Cleveland, McKinley and Roosevelt, St Clair achieved a contrasting distinction as an accomplished painter of wistful seascapes much prized today by US auction houses.

Waiting for a Train,
Lisburn Railway
Station

But my own loyalties are divided between three others, the first being General Henry Monro, that hero of the 1798 uprising; the second being the philanthropic Sir Richard Wallace, once Lisburn's landlord, and the third, a suffragette, Mrs Lilian Metge, an active member of the Belfast Womens Suffragette Society.

Blue-eyed Henry Monro, a freemason much given to hunting and shooting, was a Protestant Lisburn linen draper inspired by the freedoms sought in the American War of Independence and the French Revolution. His skills as an organiser saw him become a General leading the mainly Presbyterian and Catholic United Irishmen who were defeated by the forces of the Crown at June 1798's Battle of Ballynahinch, a martial engagement illustrated with some force in Thomas Robinson's painting of the same name. Encamped at Creevy Rocks, Saintfield, his forces encountered those of Major-General George Nugent's at Ballynahinch's Windmill Hill where the United Irishmen's inferior artillery, plus lack of battle-hardened experience, lost them the day. Seeking refuge with farmer William Holmes, Monro was – as happens so often in the history of this island's skirmishes – betrayed for pieces of silver. Imprisoned in the Huguenot church he was forced to recall that not all Lisburn's citizens had been with him, for many, fearful of uncharted progress and the destruction of the old certainties however oppressive they were, joined the opposing Orange Societies. Tried in Lisburn,

Monro was hung in Market Square, near the Market House, now the Irish Linen Centre & Lisburn Museum, in front of his own house. His wife, daughter to bleach-green owner Robert Johnston, was sequestered in her father's foursquare Georgian house at Seymour Hill, Dunmurry during these distressing proceedings. Now roughcast, this house, which had passed to the Charley family, was later developed twice into six flats; once by the NI Housing Executive and then again, after a fire, by Belfast Improved Housing.

Though a rung on the ladder broke as he stepped on it, the boul Henry continued, no doubt heavenwards, to his death after which his head was severed and impaled on a pike at the Market House to discourage those of his supporters still at large. His other remains, unmarked, lie within Lisburn Cathedral's graveyard.

One of the insurgency's most plangently stirring ballads recalls:

My name is George Campbell at the age of eighteen
I joined the United Men to strive for the green,
And many a battle I did undergo
With that hero commander, brave General Monro.

Have you heard of the Battle of Ballinahinch
Where the people oppressed rose up in defence?

When Monro left the mountains his men took the field,
And they fought for twelve hours and never did yield.

Monro being tired and in want of a sleep,
Gave a woman ten guineas his secret to keep.
But when she got the money the devil tempted her so
That she sent for the soldiers and surrendered Monro.

The army they came and surrounded the place,
And they took him to Lisburn and lodged him in jail.
And his father and mother in passing that way
Heard the very last words that their dear son did say!

"Oh, I die for my country as I fought for her cause,
And I don't fear your soldiers nor yet heed your laws.
And let every true man who hates Ireland's foe
Fight bravely for freedom like Henry Monro.

And 'twas early one morning when the sun was still low,
They murdered our hero brave General Monro,
And high o'er the Courthouse stuck his head on a spear,
For to make the United men tremble and fear.

Then up came Monro's sister, she was all dressed in green,
With a sword by her side that was well-sharped and keen.
Giving three hearty cheers, away she did go
Saying, "I'll have revenge for my brother Monro."

GILLIAN LUTTON

All ye good men who listen, just think of the fate
Of the brave men who died in the year '98.
For poor old Ireland would be free long ago
If her sons were all rebels like Henry Monro.

On August 1st 1914 Mrs Metge, then of Lisburn's Seymour Street, having taken lessons in explosives from her son in the army, went about very publicly purchasing dynamite and other ingredients from Lisburn shops. She then set about, with Dorothy Evans, planting a bomb at the east end of the Cathedral, an edifice on a now curiously confined site which dates back to Sir Fulke's 1623 private chapel, the Church of St George, a building already destroyed for the first time in the rebellion of 1641. Granted Cathedral status in 1662 by Charles II, it was destroyed for the second time in the Great Fire which had begun inside the Cathedral but which also burnt down First Lisburn Presbyterian Church, an edifice itself founded in 1687 and rebuilt in Market Square 1768.

The present Cathedral building, despite Lilian's efforts, dates mainly from 1707. For, by intent, or mishap, when the explosives did explode, they damaged little but the East Window. The conspirators, having deliberately left behind incriminating evidence, were soon, as they so desired, arrested and taken to Lisburn's now sadly demolished Courthouse which had been built in 1884 by Sir Richard Wallace. The trial was reported in little but the *Lisburn Standard* whose headlines

– 'Suffragette Antics in Lisburn Court' and 'Wild Women Released' – paled into significance in the public mind in the run up to the beginning of World War I. "There is one law for women and another for men" pleaded the guilty Lilian. But no balladeer sings for her, now, just as few enough will recall the adventures of another local hero, Brigadier General John Nicholson, mortally wounded during the Indian Mutiny of 1857, whose sabre-waving statue, with a pistol in his left hand, towers in Market Square, facing Bow Street.

Neither, unless there's a *chanson* remembered in the artistic salons of his beloved Paris, who sings the praises of Sir Richard Wallace (1818-1890)? His fountains still, literally slake the thirsts of tourists and *clochards* in the City of Light – and indeed in other cities across the globe. Few in Lisburn, a straw poll suggests, remember him: only two of his five fountains – one in Market Street, the other Castle Park – survive, but they are, sadly, dry. Let me explain: Richard, is, technically assumed to have been a bastard, either a testament to the 3rd Marquis's liason with the ballet dancer Maria Fragniania or as one of the two illegitimate sons of Viscount Beauchamp, 4th Marquis of Hertford, who was said to have fathered him when just 18 years of age. His mother, if that was the case, may well have been one of the 4th Marquis's many mistresses, Agnes Jackson, a humbly born Scots lass who went on to become *une fille du régiment* of the 10th Hussars. Whatever his maternal genetics Richard, who was known in his youth as Dick Jackson, is, in later life, shown as a small dapper man given to wearing brocaded smoking jackets and jaunty berets, plus a decidedly French moustache. He spoke with indelible traces of a Parisian accent. He also fathered a bastard son with the daughter of a French army officer. Indeed such beddings were to become an essential of the Wallace heritage, for Richard Wallace's son went on to have himself four illegitimate children.

While his reclusive father went about acquiring his magnificent collection of art, Richard became his charming agent though his father never formally acknowledged his son's provenance. On the 4th Marquis's death, Richard inherited – after a costly legal battle with Sir Hamilton Seymour – vast unentailed wealth including a Parisian château, and houses in Piccadilly plus in Berkley and Manchester Squares, along with his Lisburn properties. Living in Paris, Richard became a hero during the Prussian siege of his adopted city, funding an field ambulance, protecting the English community and distributing resources to the impoverished, thus being awarded membership of the Légion d'honneur and a baronetcy from Queen Victoria. Back in Lisburn, which he first visited in 1873, he lowered rents during the agricultural recession of the 1880s and built improved mill workers' housing 'of a superior class', while as a Conservative M.P., erecting to designs probably by William McHenry, his own stylish mansion, Castle House on Castle Street. This, which later

became the Municipal Technical College or 'The Tech' is now Lisburn's Institute of Further and Higher Education or 'LIF-HE'. Richard also built a quite Palladian Courthouse beside the Railway Station, remodelled the Market House and later founded the Assembly Rooms, plus Wallace Park, plus the 'University and Intermediate School' now known as 'Wallace High'.

Castle House, symmetrical and of red-brick in the Queen Anne style, boasts tall Georgian windows with stone eyebrows and architraves, plus a tetrastyle Doric portico. Its interior, with central hall gallery and excellent staircase, has been described as 'astonishingly grand'. Further out, as Castle Street becomes Seymour Street, lies the Georgian Infirmary established by an 1767 Act of Parliament and built by public subscriptions from the linen barons. It has recently been restored as private housing.

But back to the days of the Paris Commune and the siege of 1870-71 during which many of Paris's aqueducts were destroyed leaving the poor little to drink but alcohol. Wallace, in a typical act of extended philanthropy, commissioned the Nantes sculptor Charles-Auguste Lebourg to devise a series of cast-iron, dark green-painted, fountains whose tops were born by four supporting caryatids, the 'goddesses' of Simplicity, Temperance, Charity and Goodness, fashioned in the Renaissance style. Cast in four sizes, many of the 65 of the largest models in Paris are still in excellent working order, still dispensing cold potable water except during the coldest days of winter, and indispensable on a hot summer's day. Thus Lisburners, *en vacances*, can slake their thirsts in thanks at many Parisian venues. They include the Passage du Pont aux Biches in the 3rd arrondissement; near the Hôtel-dieu in the 4th; rue de la Bûcherie in the 5th; Pont Neuf and the Place Saint-André-des-Arts in the 6th; Chevaux de Marly, Av. des Champs-Elysées in the 8th; les Places Edith Piaf and Maurice Chevalier in the 20th. Maurice had his own, as has Brigitte Bardot. There are five *les Wallaces* in Nantes, their sculptor's birthplace, another in Toulon and others in Montréal Canada, Switzerland, Mozambique, South Africa, Jordan, New Orleans, Barcelona and Lisburn, a city whose citizens will look bemused when you ask where *les Wallaces* are before remembering the one in Castle Gardens, a public park east of the Cathedral and south of Wallace Park. Many of the park's features, including the great walled terraces, have been magnificently restored in one of the UK's largest Heritage Lottery-funded urban park regenerations.

Meanwhile, in London, Richard's widow left the marvellous family collection of ceramics, furniture, armour and paintings to the nation. Thus it is on show in one of the family homes, Hertford House, Manchester Square, London. Richard was buried, July 23, 1890, in the family vault in Père Lachaise cemetery not to far from the memorial to the Enniskillen-

A Garden Gate,
Castle Gardens

educated author, Oscar Wilde. Hertford House's collections include over 5,000 objects, amongst them many beautiful items of Sèvres porcelain and Limoges work, full suits of armour as well as the paintings. These include two Titians, four Rembrandts, three Rubenses, four Van Dycks, twenty-two Canalettos, nineteen Bouchers, masterpieces by Hooch, nine Teniers, Frans Hals' 'Laughing Cavalier, nine Murillos, two Velázquezes including the masterly 'Lady With a Fan' along with others by Thomas Gainsborough, Joshua Reynolds and Antoine Watteau and Albert Cuyp.

In Lisburn there's the Wallace memorial, close to the war memorial and erected by 'popular' subscription in 1892, in Castle Gardens, the grounds given to the town by his widow's heir, Sir John Murray Scott. The nearby canon is from the Battle of Sebastopol in the Crimean War and the one-time Lisburn Temperance Union Institute in Railway Street, whose first President was the Quaker linen magnet J. N. Nicholson, was also built on a site given to the then town by Sir Richard. Quakers were, and still are, a force in the city, their peaceful heritage, a balance in a conurbation with long military associations including Thiepval Barracks, is recalled in Friend's School.

The Religious Society Of Friends, whose 17th century followers refused to pay tithes to the established church and whose 21st century adherents believe that 'all men are equal in the sight of God and have no hierarchy' reached Lisburn from England's Cumbria with shopkeeper William Edmundson. Once a Cromwellian soldier, he so impressed John Shaw of Broad Oak that when William's purchase of three of Shaw's cows was completed at a cattle fair in 1655, Shaw gathered together his neighbours for the area's first Quaker meeting near Blaris. A thatched Meeting House, accessed from a lane off Market Square, followed three years later in the garden of George Gregson, the goldsmith who would later provide dinner for William III. Being to its leeward, the building surviving the fire of 1707 but it was replaced, on the same site in 1793, and accessed off what was then Jackson's Lane, known today as Railway Street. It too was replaced sixty years later though Gregson's garden continued to be used as the Quaker burial ground till 1899. The current Quaker Meeting House is at Prospect Hill, within the grounds of Friends' School, Lisburn's first school, an institution founded in 1774 and opened up to non-Quakers from 1880, the very year Richard Wallace also opened his first Lisburn educational establishment.

But a city, as Lisburn now is, must have a cathedral as well as castles, rebels, schoolmarms, editors, soldiers, philanthropists, museums and a market place. Sir Fulks built his first Chapel of Ease to his castle in 1632. Dedicated to St Thomas, it measured but 80ft by 25ft and boasted, probably and proudly, both tower and spire. By the time it was lost in the

Quaker Connections,
Friends' School

bloody battles of 1641 it had become the town's church, later to be rebuilt, much along the same lines but with an added balcony, in 1674.

Curiously, as both Connor's cathedral, as well as Downpatrick's, had been burnt in those very same wars, and as both had shared the same bishops, Lisburne's (viz), being geographically central, was then constituted, by Royal Charter as the Cathedral Church of the several bishoprics of the dioceses of Connor and Down on October 27th, 1662 during the term of the saintly Jeremy Taylor, Bishop of Down and Connor, Administrator of Dromore.

The conflagration of 1707 which began inside the cathedral during a divine service destroyed much of town, church, gown and crown. While the castle was never rebuilt, new founds for the cathedral were laid on 20th August 1708 while a new tax to pay for its reconstruction was laid upon the inhabitants of the parish, a cess not welcomed particularly by those whose families would rise with the United men in 1798. Buttressed externally, the building has an aisless blackstone nave with a four-storey 75ft western tower with but a slight batter. This tower, which once bore a cupola, now supports four corner pinnacles and a splendid 96ft octagonal spire which was added in 1804, its costs shared between the parishioners and the Marquis of Hertford who also gifted the clock and bells. The organ dates back to 1790. On cast-iron

columns, the galleries which, rather sadly bisect the windows and darken the interior, were added in 1824. The east window, Lilian Metge's if you like, was replaced in 1950 by one to the Barbour family. More melodramatically two dashing memorial tablets recall battles past: one by Edward Smyth commemorates sailor William Dobbs, the other, by J. H. Foley is to General Nicholson. Since then the addition of many changes, great and small, have, at the time of their introduction, divided the congregation of this small and, truthfully, unremarkable parish church hemmed in as it is between Castle Street, Market Square, Bridge Street and Queen's Road.

More importantly there were those who argued that Charles II's chapter recognising the building as a cathedral had never been properly enacted. For it had received neither the sanction of Parliament, nor the Royal Seal. All was assumed to have been resolved by a Bill of Recognition passed at the General Synod of the Church of Ireland in 1952. But enough grey areas remain to engage those who would debate the number of angels who could dance on the head of a pin. Here is a parish church with Rector, Dean and Chapter though – while the members of the chapter are parish priests of the diocese – the offices of Dean of Connor and Rector of Christ Church remain separate. For the Dean's title is an honorary one while the Chapter is styled after The Dean and Chapter of St Saviour, Connor, in the Cathedral of Christ Church, Lisburn. Thus, arguably, Belfast's St Anne's Cathe-

Union Bridge

dral, plus the cathedral churches of Dromore and Downpatrick, plus the ex-cathedral Church of St Saviour at Connor, were not really affected by the Bill of 1952.

To the still confused it may be useful to know that Connor's once-upon-a-time Cathedral Church of St Saviour, taking its name from the Irish word *connere* – meaning the 'hounds' oak wood' – is to be found in a tiny village of the same name in county Antrim, not county Down. That is 8km south of Ballymena, where in 1315 Edward – brother to Robert the Bruce – claiming the kingship of Ireland, defeated the Anglo-Normans under Richard de Burgh, Earl of Ulster. Burnt by Edward's Scots soldiery, neither cathedral nor church ever regained their previous status. Architecturally plain and single-chambered, its other fame, for some, rests in the fact that the satirist Jonathan Swift, author of Gulliver's Travels and later Dean of St Patrick's Cathedral in Dublin, preached there on 28th April 1695, reading the service of his appointment as Prebendary of Kilroot.

In the city's Hertford Arms you might sup a pint of the 'black-stuff', or at the Hilden Brewery one of its real ales, and debate the eternal pub-quiz question: did Louis Crommelin settle for Lisburn because he saw on a map that the nearby town of Hillsborough had previously been called, by the indigenous Irish, *Crom ghlinn*, spoken near enough as Crommelin, the Crooked Glen?

A number of the linen family houses were built farther from the river at Dunmurry, inspired by the opening Ulster Railway Company's line to Lisburn. Built for the Charley family, Conway, which was named for Lord Conway, one of the titles of the local landowner the Marquess of Hertford, was later leased to the Bishop of Down, Conor and Dromore before being sold to the Barbours of Hilden. A scan of the family tree of the Barbours is more than instructive for having experienced the unreliability of Scottish yarns for their mills in Paisley and thus decided to add Irish material to the twists, John Barbour, in 1783 built a thread mill, Barbour's Linen Thread Mill, complete with workers' houses and bleach green in a village he established and called The Plantation, south east of Lisburn. These works were succeeded by those at Hilden before expanding into America and becoming the largest manufacturer of tailor's and shoemaker's threads in the world. John's son John continued to live at thee-bay, three-storey Plantation House but another son, William, moved on, constructing the 5-bay hipped-roofed Irish Georgian Hilden House in 1824, having knocked down the home of the Huguenot bleach-green developer Samuel de la Cherois.

Briefly William and his wife Eliza had lived first at Bridge End and then in Castle Street, Lisburn but William's children lived at Hilden and then at Conway and at Danesfort off Belfast's Malone Road, this last a house which became the offices of the province's electricity supply company, NI Electricity.

Linen's Legacy,
Hilden House

GILLIAN LUTTON

*The Mill at the End of
the Road,
Hilden*

Further Barbour generations lived in Hilden, in Strathearne (now Hunterhouse College), the demolished 'The Fort', site of Fort Hill Girls' School – Grove Green, overlooking the Lagan, in Clonmore at Lambeg, also now destroyed, plus Dunanin on the Malone Road and in Victorian Conway which became an hotel before it too was lost. The Barbour family mausoleum in Lambeg Parish Church is like that of the Wolfendens, a Listed building. Hilden House's stables became the Hilden Brewery late in the 20th century.

 The Lagan Valley Regional Park, to which the author must declare a personal connection, is, in itself, the river's most user-friendly advocate, even though, somewhat perversely, the LVRP's current literature maps the flow back-to-front as it were, placing North, against all convention, at the bottom of the page rather than at the top. Thus it illustrates a Lagan River and its Lagan Navigation Canal which would appear to begin at Belfast's Stranmillis and meander east to west - rather as in real life west to east - ending up after Lisburn, just past the confluence with the Ravarnet River at Union Locks.

The logic, if that's the correct word, would seem to be that the majority of walkers, cyclists and canoeists traversing along or between the towpaths will begin their journeys in Belfast rather than in Lisburn's new City. Bearing this convolution in mind and reading the Lock numbers from Number 1, the now filled-in Molly Ward's, named for the family whose lock-keeper's cottage stood on the site of the Stranmillis Boat Club, right up to Numbers 14 -17, the Union Locks, the Park is one of Ulster's most civilised delights. The Union Locks also mark the beginning of the 'Lagan and Lough Cycle Way' which, punctuated by National Cycle Network mileposts and signed access points, doubles with the Lagan Towpath right into Belfast, past Belvoir Park at 10 miles, and hence along the docks and on to Whiteabbey and Jordanstown's Loughshore Park, a total pedal of over 20 miles.

A tempting diversion though, might be first be to trace the course of one of the Lagan's tributaries, the Ravarnet, which joins its big sister at the Park's western boundary having meandered west and north from Ballinahinch past Saintfield and Baileysmills to run between the villages of Ravarnet and Duneight before reaching the Lagan. This last has village has a prized 12th century Norman motte and bailey fortification.

A Footbridge over the Navigation, or, upstream of the Ravarnet tributary, where 3-arched Moore's Bridge, built of sandstone topped with black-stone parapets in 1824 for the Lisburn-Hillsborough Turnpike as it runs into Old Warren Nature Trail, both give access to where the flight of the Union Locks, Nos 14 - 17 with their 26ft drop brokered the difference of levels between canal and river.

The 13th Lock, Betty Hogg's, named as to custom after its lock-keeper, is upstream of Hogg's Weir whose mill race is still just in evidence, here and there, beside the towpath running downstream to Lisburn. Hannah's Lock, Lock 12, faithfully restored alongside the Island Arts Centre, is an integral part of the elegantly landscaped Lagan Valley Island development complex with its outdoor sculpture bark, berthing for a motor-driven pastiche canal boat, Council Chambers, riverside bistro and seasonal midstream fountain which, just upstream of what was previously called Vitriol Island complete with spinning mill and bleach manufacturing works, cools summer's breezes.

A rearrangement of the towpath's route, which once ran along Canal Street to Union Bridge, but which now veers northeast of the Island, disturbs few bar industrial archaeologists. Downstream of the Blue Bridge comes Scott's Lock, no. 11, where three watercourses, canal, millrace and river, run in parallel, upstream of Hilden Bridge, itself the location of the 10th Lock beside the massive Hilden Mill, adjacent to one of Ulster's few microbreweries, Hilden, a delightful institution running its own ale festival and restaurant. At the Mill Quay, barge mooring rings survive.

Further downstream, below where the Tullymacross Road crosses over the Lambeg Iron Suspension Bridge, is the site of the 9th Lock, dominated once by the Lambeg Bleach Works whose situation, and the bleach green which had preceded them in 1626, were dictated by the presence of a massive underground freshwater aquifer. From the parklands of Aberdelghy Lands you could watch golfers's foursomes, but Lambeg itself is better known now through the name of the Lambeg Drum, a massive goatskin-headed 'man o' war' now associated with the Protestant Orange Order and their province-wide 12th of July marches commemorating 1690's Battle of the Boyne. In past centuries a drum's beat was all that could be heard carrying marching orders through the smoke of ordnance above the boom of canon and musket, plus the screams of the maimed. For the instrument's contemporary fans, competitive summer evening drumming matches at country crossroads, where combatants tune their skins and then blatter with Malacca canes, man to man, in many decibel rhythms of ever increasing rapidity, are the very height of their culture.

Whatever one's persuasion, few could or would contend that there is not a particular martial magic to the distant resonant rhythm of a Lambeg, heard before first breaching a far away misty hilltop, accompanied by the spare accompaniment of a sole B flat fife. Once the Lambeg was beaten by the men of the Protestant Orange Order as well as the Catholic Ancient Order of Hibernians, but approach them now, till the two players are close enough to taste the sweat of conflict and you'll discern only the iconic images of King Billy's accoutrements, his white charger and his plumed hat, painted on the drum's circumference.

East of Lambeg, comes a rash of bridges The first is basalt and sandstone Wolfenden's with its five river – and another four flood – arches, with cutwaters facing both upstream and downstream. It was first recorded in Sir William Petty's Down Survey of 1657. The second is Ballyskeagh's High Bridge, which crosses, variously, the straight canal and the meandering river. East of Wolfenden's are the sporting delights of Ballyskeagh or Thorntown from the Irish, its golf centre, greyhound track and the new Grosvenor Stadium home to the once peripatetic Distillery Football Club. This was first formed in 1880 by the workers in Dunville's Royal Irish Distillery in Belfast. They played at Daisy Hill, then Broadway, and later York Park. Once a major force in European soccer, in 1889 they beat Newtown Heath, a club which later morphed, renamed, as Manchester United. Distillery drew 3-3 with Benfica in 1963. Driven from Grosvenor Park by the 'Troubles' they've played at Ballskeagh since 1980 and are now officially known as Lisburn Distillery F.C.

Paper manufacturer Abraham Wolfenden of Lambeg House, a man who'd left Germany for Ireland at the request of the Duke of Ormonde, became the master of these island's finest quality woollen blankets. He also, in 1690, played host to King William when the Protestant hero stopped to speak to a

GILLIAN COTTON

GILLIAN CUTTERS

Many Arches,
Lambeg Bridge

Huguenot couple, René and Madame Bulmer. Abraham supplied wood to repair one of the royal wagons when it broke down crossing the ford where the bridge now stands. One hundred and thirty years later, a personal carriage of a member of Russia's Royal household suffered a similar disaster on the very same spot. Heightened, remodelled and extended to suit the more sophisticated society of 1760, and by then called Harmony Hill, the house was again reordered in 1860 and in 1900. Lambeg's Lagan Lodge, with its Georgian glazing and half-round, three storey, staircase annexe, was also built for the Wolfenden family, probably as the mill manager's house known as Primrose Cottage, on the site of an antique travellers' inn. Overlooking the Lagan and home to a distinguished conservation architect, Chrome Hill as it was first named by the 19th century muslin printer Richard Niven – an entrepreneur who perfected the use of bichromates to fix his colours – is one of the valley's most charming houses with, in the garden, trees said to have been twinned together by the preacher John Wesley.

But it is at Ballyskeagh's sandstone arches, steps and remaining lock house, that the traveller glimpses the architectural merit of the works of Thomas Omer, the Navigation's engineer. One further bridge, the New Footbridge, comes before the 8th Lock, itself flanked on the south by McIlroy Park, named for that elegant soccer midfielder, Lambeg-born Jimmy McIlroy, hero of Burnley F.C.'s English League Cham-

pionship. Ramblers then face another footbridge, the green Ramblers' Bridge, which crosses over the island and both canal and river below Seymour Hill Housing Estate to the north-east, Ballyskeagh Riverside Park to the south-west. The M1 blocks the canal but its underpass leads the towpath to the 7th Lock, McQuiston's, with its nearby arched bridge and ruined lock house.

Lychgate at Drumbeg
Church

Continuing downstream on the southern riverbank, with the Sir Thomas and Lady Dixon Park across the water and from that public Park's bridge, upstream of the Drumbridge, there are fine views of the 6th Lock, The Drum, complete with its bollards and restored lock house. St Patrick's Church of Ireland, which dates its various versions back to 1303, comes complete with a lynch-gate, a graveyard of Linen barons much visited by the English poet Philip Larkin when he worked in the Library at Queen's University, plus a fallen memorial to James Haddock who, having died intestate had, it is recorded, appeared in court four years later in dramatically ghostly form to right his executor's illegal machinations. A fine portrait of tall dark and handsome John McCance hangs in the Ulster Museum in the Laganside's Botanic Gardens while his memorial, which enhances the burial grounds, is but one of the memories of stone. Others, more humble, mark the resting placed of the more humble workers from Thompson's Dyeworks, built where The Hermitage now stands. Originally a bleach green and buckling house for Hamilton Maxwell's Dutch bleachers it was soon replaced, in 1725, by a beetling mill powered by the waters of the Lagan. Drum House, where

the Maxwells lived, dates from the late 17th century, but it became the property of Miss Elizabeth Moore, treasurer of Belfast's Ragged School and was remodelled in the 1880s by the Belfast drapers and milliners, the Arnott family.

Dixon Park, much promoted for its regimented rose trials, extends its rolling acres, home to the pigmy shrew and a veritable cornucopia of edible fungi, right down to the riverside. The Park's principal building, Wilmont, was originally designed in 1760 for William Stewart of Ballydrain who established his extensive linen bleach greens both within his 108 Irish acres as well as at Edenderry, Newforge, Dunmurry and Lambeg. It was rebuilt in 1860 as a curious double-mansion for the Northern Bank's director James Bristow and his son James Thompson Bristow, a confection dismissed by the late Lord Glentoran as 'a large semi-detached'. Bristow sold to R. H. S. Reade, later Chairman of the York Street Flax Spinning Company who added the estate's Lisburn Gate Lodge before selling it on to one of his Board members, Sir Thomas Dixon. In 1963 it became Belfast Corporation property, an 'old peoples' home', and an avant garde art space. It now rests, empty, unlike Ballydrain – now Malone Golf Clubhouse – which, having gone through various architectural styles since 1608 was, in its Tudor Revival phase owned by John Barbour Morrison of the massive Ulster Spinning Company, an enterprise itself owned by the Morrison, Mackie and Metcalf families.

Indeed, towards the end of the last century these lower reaches of the Lagan on the outskirts of the city were an increasingly favoured location for the grand piles of the Linen Barons.

Finaghy House, originally Ballyfinaghy House was home to the Charleys, a Lancashire linen dynasty, originally named Chorley, who had fled England's Jacobite Rebellion and intermarried with the neighbouring linen barons, the Wolfendens, McCances, Richardsons, Herdmans, Riddells, Reades and Duffins. Now, more modest and renamed Faith House, a home for senior citizens, its Charley armorial bearings still decorate the gables. The fate of the unusual revolving fireplace, which served, alternatively, drawing room and dining room, is unrecorded.

Georgian Belvedere, a rather bland though B1 listed three-bay house with a Tuscan porch, on the Ballylesson Road and the Lagan as its western boundary, was purchased by the son of a Lisburn tanner, James Watson Hull, who made a fortune in the East India Company and was known as the Nabob who ultimately, Lord Downshire having declined the honour, paid for the building of Drumbo's new church. Belvedere passed into the hands of the Duncan family, bleachers by trade, before eventually coming, in 1948, into the possession of Brigadier Broadhurst, an Arabist who was a member of the Beersheba Camelry, Equerry to King Abdullah of Jordan, Chief of Staff to both Glubb Pasha and the Arab Union and once a familiar liberally patrician pundit on Ulster Television in the 1960s. His family sold it to Gordon Mackie of James Mackie & Sons Ltd. in 1993. Seymour Hill, another large and square Georgian house facing the Lagan at Dunmurry,

A Seat in the Shade,
Lady Dixon Park

with the Derriaghy River whose mill races once powered linen factory machinery, feeding its lake, was owned by the Charley family until acquired by the Northern Ireland Housing Trust in its first vesting order just after the end of WWII. Though firebombed and vandalised, its listed section was restored by Belfast Improved Housing Association Ltd. and reopened by Colonel W.R.H. Charley, OBE, JP, DL on 12th October 1990. Glenmore House, originally named Lambeg House, was built for Lord Conway who modestly described it as 'The Lord's House'. It was purchased by a bleacher John Williamson who persuaded the Trustees of the Linen Board to pass a bye law in 1762 guaranteeing the qualities of brown linens, a measure so unpopular that four hundred weavers marched on his house, breaking its windows before being dispersed by Lord Hillsborough's troops. Glenmore was home to the Linen Industry Research Association from 1909-1993 when it was sold to property developers.

Georgian Willowdale, off the Ballybog Road and part of the Charley estate since 1820, was previously called Laganvale. Phoenix Lodge, now gone, had been home to Helen Barbour, wife to Thomas Andrews who went down with his controversially designed liner, the Titanic. Woodburn House had been home the Charleys, as was Warren House, later lived in by rogue playboy motor manufacturer John Zachary De Lorean whose 9,200 gull-winged DMC-12 stainless steel Renault V6-engined cars both echoed an earlier Mer-

cedes and drained off £100m of British government money into a never fully explored 'black hole'. Huntley, built for the Hunters of Dunmurry House, later bleach green merchants brought from Scotland by Cromwell, had also been a Charley home till sold to G. H. Bryson of Spence Bryson. Dunmurry House became Housing Executive flats but the Hunter legacy is preserved in both Hunterhouse College established at Strathearne House, a former Barbour linen house and in another Hunter house, Duneight on the banks of the Ravarnet tributary. Glenburn, off the townland of Old Forge on the banks of the Glen River, was built by a Wolfenden and is now Belfast Bible College. Rathmore House, built for linen mill steam-engine manufacturer Victor Coates, is now also a school.

But back to below Drumbeg where the towpath, now on the north bank, leads to the wetlands around a further island which divides canal from river approaching the 5th Lock, until the two courses are reunited at the Footbridge by the 4th Lock at the river's Eel Weir. To the north lie the manicured hectares of Barnett's Demesne and Malone Golf Club; to the south, in the townland of Ballynahatty, the Giant's Ring, a great 600ft diameter 12ft high circular bank, built of stone and gravel. Though the enclosure was once used for horseracing with the bank but an alfresco grandstand, just a mite off its centre lies its presumably primary mission, the 'Druid's Grave' a basalt dolmen of five uprights and a capstone under

Stones in Snow,
Giant's Ring

GILLIAN LITTON

which were found much cremated bone. The nearby circular rath, 300ft in diameter, on Fort Hill in Ballylesson or the Townland of Little Forts, and encroached on by housing, is called locally Farrell's Fort.

Gilchrist's Bridge, named for the bureaucrat credited as the Lagan Valley Regional Park's founder, sits upstream of what was once a 19th century mill village, Edenderry, where John Shaw Brown's works and his workers produced Shamrock Damask. Opposite it is the Mary Peters Track, named for Ulster's Golden Girl of athletics, an Olympic Pentathlon Gold Medallist. Downstream, an Ulster Wildlife Trust Nature Reserve rings with the voices of stock-doves, plus song and mistle thrush. Broad-leaved *helleborines* will, in season, be apparent enough, as will the red-billed blackish moor hen, *Gallinuala chloropus*, with its throaty 'kurruk' or the high-pitched 'pitt' of the white-billed slate-black coot, bandicoot to some, baldycoot to others, *Fulica atra* to ornithologists. But sighting the shy, rare and elusive water rail, *Rallus aquaticus*, an olive-brown bird with a grey breast, will test the impatient's patience till it gives one of its loud, explosive pig-like squeals from deep in the rushes and reeds.

The Minnowburn, a Lagan tributary mentioned in the rhyming – and deceptively heroic – memoirs of Julius McCullough Lecky Craig, Ulster's counterpart to the lugubrious Scots poet William Topaz McGonagall, joins the southern shore at the

Minnowburn Bridge alongside the National Trust's stately Minnowburn Beeches whose Freddy's Steps, named for their creator Frederick Russell, lead steeply up to Terrace Hill Garden thus affording the fine vistas of Minnowburn Pond and Sandpit Field where the sports centre's pitches have given way to those on another public park, Barnett's Demesne. This is named for William Barnett and with its springtime screeds of rare daffodils, its darting grey and red squirrels, its wildflower meadows flickering in summer with meadow-brown, ringed, green-veined-white and small-copper butterflies, its oak and beech wood it can be a delight for early risers enjoying a dawn chorus of chiff-chaff and blackcap wary surely of the Park's long-eared owls while contrasting with the harsher cry of the jay when the badgers have returned to their sets.

Upstream, the Minnow Burn itself becomes known as Purdy's Burn descending, under Purdysburn Bridge, the Black Bridge and the Crooked Bridge from the south-west at Carryduff, Black Harry's Place in Irish, past Knockbracken Mental Health Services, better known to past generations as Purdysburn Asylum. A further small tributary flows into the Lagan from Galwally Lake's private Bird Sanctuary. Much-restored Malone House, surrounded by fey animist woodland sculptures, was built for William Wallace Legge in the 1820s and came into Belfast city's ownership during WWII. Its restaurant feeds conferences when not proffering tea and scones to ladies admiring the work of Sunday painters in the upstairs art gallery.

Shaw's Bridge, overlooked by The Weir, a house built for the Lisburn-born linen magnate Thomas Somerset, is now but a byway supplanted by a modern structure. It was constructed of wood during 1655 by Captain John Shaw to ordnance Oliver Cromwell's Army Train. Rebuilt in stone 1698 and again, this time as a five arched structure, in 1709, it is much beloved by Belfast's citizens whether they admire or decry the New Model Army's historic and bloody march through Ireland. From there canoeists descend the mini-rapids to Clement Wilson Park while kingfishers flash and grey-wagtails wag amongst the dipping swallows and swifts while thinking nought about the former New Forge millrace filled in by WWII air-raid shelter rubble and hence now called the Burma Road. Who indeed recalls Clement himself whose fruit-canning enterprises – which had replaced wooden clog-making workshops – created Ulster's first factory garden, the kernel of the present Council-owned Park. The Wilson Park has its own Bridge before the Red Footbridge crosses river and canal at the 3rd Lock, McLeave's, complete with its lock-keeper's cottage, downstream of which lies Belvoir Park Forest, an estate laid out in 1740 by Arthur Hill who also designed its Manor House on what was once Lord Deramore's estate.

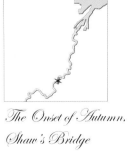

The Onset of Autumn,

Shaw's Bridge

Belvoir, pronounced near enough as Beaver, fittingly has a Forest of Belfast Information Point which might supply all the information ever required about the Park's agile red and grey squirrels, munching rabbits, water's edge rats plus their predators, the Irish stoat and the foxes around the greens in the Park's Golf Club. Patience is rewarded with nocturnal badgers, and otters by Moreland's Meadow and at the Red Bridges. Predacious long-eared owls hunt the nocturnal long-tailed field mice, plus the tiny and ferocious pigmy shrew.

Who knows but the bank vole may be there too. Certainly walkers say they have spotted another mammal, the seal, searching for an elusive salmon, climbing over the Stranmillis Weir which is the upstream boundary for tidal salt water.

But even those with more specialised interests will be find it difficult to distinguish one night-flying bat, a pipistrell say, from another; tips would include the information that those balleting over the Lagan's waters are probably Daubenton's, that those flying straight above the trees are mainly Leisler's, and that those with very big ears are Long-Eared. The raptors chasing the bats are usually either sparrow-hawks or kestrels. Buzzards too prey on lesser creatures in the Park.

More to a family's fancy may well be the flocks of winter waxwings along Belvoir Drive, the numerous crossbills, the huge gatherings of lesser redpolls, blackcap warblers, siskins, bramblings, plus the expected garden species of blue, coal, great and long-tailed tits, greenfinches and chaffinches, plus blackbirds and robins.

Kingfishers hole up in the rivers' banks, herons fish for eels, cormorants stake out the Minnowburn near where the dippers nest. Galwally lake is the place to watch coot and moor hen, water rail and little grebe, mallard, pochard and tufted-duck. Nearer to the ground the plaited snail, *Spermodea lamellata,* plus the English chrysalis snail, *Leiostyla anglica,* hide under the litter of oak and beech; the Pyrenean glass snail, *Semilimax pyrenaicus,* shelters under the alder. A dozen species of slug are there for the finding, ranging from the warty-looking hedgehog slug, *Arion intermedius,* the larger Inishowen slug *Arion owenii,* the big black *Arion ater,* the ash-black *Limax cinereoniger* and the tiger slug *Limax maximus,* to the Irish yellow-blotched slug *Limax maculatus* feeding on lichen.

More palatable, and identifiable with surety on walks arranged through the Northern Ireland Fungus Group which will help the visitor sort out their edible ceps and penny buns from the deadly Destroying Angel *Amanita virosa* and the hallucinatory Fly Agaric *Amanita muscaria* plus the definitely unpleasant Snakeskin Agaric *Amanita inaurata,* Panther Cap *Amanita pantherens* and the Blusher *Amanita rubescens.*

Belvoir, which stretches downstream from Ardnavally, home to the US Consul General, around the housing estate via Big Wood, Corbie Wood, Arboretum and Motte to the golf course, dates back over 350 years to its founding as an estate by Arthur Hill who encircled his new woodland mansion with 600 acres of pleasure walks and glasshouses with a five kilometre long wall. Surviving the uprising of 1798, the Great Wind of 1839 and the Famine, the costs of managing the estate after WWI, by which time it had passed into the hands of, first Thomas Bateson – later Lord Deramore – of Moira who added a porch designed by W. J. Barrie and bearing the Bateson crest of bat's wings, and was then leased in 1900 to Walter Wilson the publicity-shy fourth partner, with Pirrie, of Harland and Wolff, led to the house emptying after it was leased to Sir James Johnston, Lord Mayor of Belfast 1917-18. Demolished in 1961, its last caretaker was Thomas Chesney, surely my distant relative? The Bateson heraldic bats derived from the family's name Bates Son, as did their motto, *Nocte Volamus* or 'We fly by night'.

Today Belvoir is the home 130 native oaks, 47 beech, 18 horse chestnuts, 15 sycamores, 14 lime, 5 yew, 4 ash, 4 Turkey oak, 3 Lucombe oak, 3 sweet chestnut and one holm oak have girths of more than three metres. One native oak reaches around three times that whilst one in Corbie wood has been dated by Queen's University's Palaeoecology Centre as existing from AD 1642. Examination of stumps on the Lagan's bed near Shaw's Bridge puts them as having been felled in 1617, predating Captain Shaw's construction by 37 years.

Moyses Hill, my ancestor, had built forts on the Lagan's banks at Malone and Stranmillis before one of his descendants built his mansion at Hillsborough and an other, Arthur Hill, built Belvoir House and created its game reserves in the 1730s while his mother paid for the construction of Knockbreda Church. Paintings from the 1750s show a magnificent two (and later three) storey, seven bay, mansion with views of Cave Hill and the Long Bridge overlooking Corbie Wood and the river Lagan. Andrew Nichol's famous painting, from Newtonbreda Churchyard, recalls a different panorama during Bateson's days while Joseph Molloy's 1830 watercolour of Belvoir House itself, with leisure fishermen on the river, speaks of confident riches and bosky pleasures. Wealthy by inheritance, Arthur Hill had become 1st Viscount Dungannon and Chancellor of the Exchequer whilst one of his daughters, Anne, gave birth to many children one of whom grew up to be Arthur Wellesley, the Duke of Wellington. Thus your humble scribe becomes a distant relative of the Iron Duke.

While Anne lived just at downstream Annadale House, which leant its site, its name and the Duke's motto *virtus fortunae comes* or 'fortune favours the brave' to Annadale School (now Wellington College) till lately across the river from the rowing, bowling and boat clubs, the Duke played, as a boy, at

Snow in the Meadow,
Belvoir Park

Belvoir. More intriguingly the Duke's birthplace has never been proven, with Dublin historians favouring Dublin, and some Lagansiders still putting the case for Annadale.

The sign-posted walks in Lagan Meadows Local Nature Reserve, accessed from the left bank across the river, or from Malone Road's Deramore Drive, direct the flâneur to Lester's Dam, the source of the city's first water supply 200 years ago which ran through holding ponds in Botanic Gardens. They also point to the riches of Lagan Meadows' wood anemones, flag iris, and wild orchids. Snipe dart, tree-creepers creep and herons feed on marsh's eels and frogs. In summer grazing cattle low over Moreland's Meadow, once an island cut off by a canal cut, but now linked to the towpath by a small bridge near the 2nd Lock, Mickey Taylor's. The 1st Lock, Molly Ward's named for the lock-keeper who, with her watchmaker husband William, lived a quarter of a mile upstream in an 18th century tavern of which no trace remains. Coxs and scullers will tell you however, over a pint in its bar, that their Boat Club stands on the very spot. Coarse fishermen, maggoting for rudd, perch and spinning for pike, will claim, also against all the evidence, that Molly's stood on Hay Island. There are drinkers from nearby Stranmillis University College, found supping in the Cutters' Wharf pub, south of the Governor's Bridge, who'll also claim to be drinking where Moll pulled the pints.

Just downstream of the Governor's Bridge, a 1970s construct, is the Lyric Players Theatre where Liam 'Oscar Schindler' Neeson first strode the Boards. Just downstream spread the boot-shaped and riparian and once 'Royal' Botanic Gardens with their splendid Tropical Ravine plus their marvellous Palm House. This latter was fashioned by Dublin ironmaster Richard Turner and designed by Sir Charles Lanyon, the corrupt politician, philanderer and the architect of so many of Belfast's most masterly buildings. To port, off the stern, stands first the Ulster Museum and Friar's Bush Graveyard, the city's oldest Christian site, close to the dreaming spires of the Lanyon-designed Queen's University quadrangle, off, as it were, the prow.

Many of the early Botanic Gardens' exotic plants were shipped from far and away, collected by the younger sons of toffs and rectors, sustained on their long journeys by being cosseted sealed inside Wardian cases, glass domes where their transpired water vapours condensed inside the glass covers and ran back down into the soil. Invented by Dr Ward, their expeditious qualities were celebrated by the Belfast Wardian Society, the first such body in the British Isles.

Once upon a time the Gardens boasted birds donated by the Charley linen family of Seymour Hill and Harland and Wolff's Lord Pirrie while money-making fêtes offered submarine explosions and balloon ascents with gas supplied and

A Quiet Corner,
Palm House, Botanic
Gardens

piped from the Belfast Gaswords downstream. One such daring spectacle came complete with a lady parachutist, vouched 'most respectable' before the Corporation would permit even a flash of her Victorian ankle. Whilst once only selected subscribers, and later 'respectable tradesmen and their families' had been gifted admission, the 'lower orders' were later admitted when the Garden's company which had been set up to serve God, was forced to conjoin with Mammon. Not everyone approved: 'grossly indecent' goings on were reported amongst the bushes, even during church-going hours. The mounted 5th Dragoon Guards gave barebacked wrestling displays and the Gardens' first botanist was appointed. He was Thomas Drummond, the naturalist on one of Sir John Franklin's voyages to find the North-West passage through the Arctic – now, as likely as not, the Garden's concert might be by Van Morrison.

Towards the north-west corner of the Gardens, shaded by the Pinetum, and across Stranmillis Road from the Conor Café, an artists' haunt built where one of the province's best loved painters had his studio, stands the Ulster Museum.

The Museum, which of course remembers Belfast's industrial heritage which gave the world the Titanic also houses the treasures of a much earlier ship, the galleas Girona of the Spanish Armada, which, having survived attacks by the English navy, and the atrocious storms of the time, floundered off the province's northern coast. As well as the venue's immense scientific and accessible ecological resources are its art galleries, Belfast's largest, where, alongside temporary exhibitions you'll usually find a selection of Conor's shipyard workers and his inevitably smiling poor, but also of Dan O'Neill's mythic women, Gerard Dillon's quirky remembrances of artists' larks, Sir John Lavery's luminous but fawning portraits and Paul Henry's comforting posterised impressions of Ireland's west. In its vaults are many canvases telling the Lagan's history.

Just downstream of the Lyric, after the King's Bridge, this island's first reinforced concrete bridge built in 1910, along the Stranmillis Embankment stands a group of cottages, Southview Cottages, below 'Horsey Hill' where horses paused before tackling the causeway which would have taken them across to what's now Ormeau Park over open ground now housed with streets named for the declining Empire's Indian affrays, Delhi, Baroda, Burmah and Candahar. Behind Southview Cottages lies the 'Holy Land' a grid of redbrick terraces named Cairo, Damascus, Palestine and Carmel currently let to Queen's University's students. Downstream again lay the city's gasworks, swept away for a series of uncoordinated commercial developments where only the spare cubed and domed Meter House, plus the gaswork's offices which had been described as having the most impressive redbrick façade in these island, speak of its former robust glories. Across the Ormeau

Road, off Donegall Pass, the streets are named for the elms, oaks, pines and walnuts of the 18th century's Cromack Wood, while, across the pass St Mary Magdalen's precursor reserved a gallery for 'erring and repentant females' who survived its once notorious Magdalene Asylum.

Vestiges of McConnell's Weir, which enhanced rather than removed the Lagan's silting, remain north of the Ormeau Bridge, built 1815, rebuilt 1863, along with those of Cromac Lock, once the river's upriver first, near Hauliers' Way and Potters' Quay before the Albert Bridge.

Belfast's lands, originally gifted to the English adventurer Sir James Chichester by James I in the 17th century, lay within the estates of his successors, the various Earls of Donegall well into the mid-19th century. When the 5th Earl and 1st Marquis, died in 1799 he was succeeded by his son, thirty year-old George Augustus, the second Marquis, a charmer who ran up such staggering gambling debts that, after his death in 1844, most of the city had to be sold to its inhabitants through the Incumbered Estates Court. In 1807, the Donegalls, living frugally in what was then the corner of Linenhall Street and Donegall Square, having found themselves too poor to purchase even a new doorcase, moved goods and chattels, via the Long Bridge at the end of Anne Street, to Ormeau Cottage in the townland of Ballynafeigh in what has since become public Ormeau Park, complete with its playing fields, indoor tennis courts, bowling greens, gymnasium and public golf course.

The word Ormeau, as was the fashion of the time, was of French origin, taken from the two words, *orme*, meaning elm and *eau*, meaning water: thus Elms-by-the-Water. Later the Donegalls improved their Ormeau Demesne and enlarged the farmhouse to a grand mock Tudor Ormeau House around 1830, completing it with a pheasantry and a racing stud breeding horses for the Marquis's racecourse. Haypark Avenue, nearby, across the Ormeau Road, recalls its working farm. The pillars to the grand gates onto the Ravenhill Road were topped with gilt coronets and the family's crest of a heron about to swallow a struggling eel. The building of the Ormeau Bridge in 1815 did not affect their privileged style though while in 1812 'every brick in Belfast was owned by Lord Donegall' hardly one was his by 1832.

Belfast's citizens, who unlike the denizens of other maritime/riparian cities have no collective name such as Belfasters or Belfastians to match those of Dubliners, Glaswegians or Londoners, are currently facing the dilemma as to how to remember what some might call the Lagan's most famous product – the ill-fated passenger liner HMS Titanic, built in the city's once world-revered shipyard, Harland and Wolff.

Rain in the Park,
Ormeau Park

Yes there are a number of Titanic Societies, Titanic Dinners, Titanic Conferences and a developers' cash cow, the recently defined Titanic Quarter, the transformation of 75 brownfield hectares of Queen's Island into a complex of bland high-rise apartments and a marina in the Abercorn Basin, plus an internationally branded hotel, an elusive 'signature building', plus a new venue for BIFHE, the Belfast Institute of Further and Higher Education.

The Titanic's actual heritage would appear to be slight. Harland and Wolff's iconic cranes, Samson and Goliath (or Samson and Dehlila as some prefer) whose heights dwarfed the previous Arrol gantries, and which were erected more then a century and a half after the liner's loss, are indeed protected by their 'listed' status as maybe will be the shipyard's arcane steam cranes while the ultimate fate of vast slipways – from which the Titanic, and its equally ill-fated White Star Line sister ship the Olympic were launched – remains in the balance. The site's most magnificent interior, that of the Harland and Wolff drawing office will become an interpretative centre while the massive Paint Hall, has, due to its weighty construction, become soundproofed film studio. A lobby of conservationists, public and private, fear an 'olde worlde pastiche', worrying that, barring the recent rescue and reclamation of the Nomadic, a tender which ferried passengers from Southampton out to the liner, little will be retained bar a smattering of bollards, rail-lines and cobbled walkways, picturesquely outlining the Hamilton, Thompson and Alexander Dry and Graving Docks.

Certainly the city's recent riparian regeneration, apart from its Waterfront Hall, a building whose interior appears to owe much to Finland's Tampere Concert Hall, pales into architectural significance when compared with world class achievements of the two Spanish provincial capitals of Bilbao and Valencia. For the Basques, Frank Ghery's Guggenheim Museum heralded an environmentally architect-led integrated makeover which transposed a post-industrial shipyard wasteland into one of Europe's most popular weekend break destinations. For the Valencians, their shipyards were replaced by Sebastian Calatrava's limestone City of Arts and Sciences, a series of organically shaped buildings affording an enhancing aesthetic and intellectual experience which is transforming the city's fortunes.

Belfast, for its sins, gained an untidy string of unlovely waterside apartments running, with interruptions, from Stranmillis to the sea, its only other signature building being the Odyssey, a brash entertainment mall in US-mode hosting ten-pin bowling, IMAX cinema, ice-hockey clashes and 10,000 seater travelling music shows alongside the inventively interactive and child-friendly W5. While the Science Centre may foster innovation, its outward skin offers only the mundane.

Reflections of a City,
Waterfront Hall

– Belfast's promised 'Titanic Signature project' has a lot riding on it.

Across Donegall Square East from the Titanic Memorial, once stood showrooms for Dromore-born Harry Ferguson, pioneer aviator, car manufacturer and designer of the iconic 'Fergie' tractor. Down May Street, past its Presbyterian Church where, like the city's St Anne's Cathedral in Donegall Street, Titanic memorial services were held, stood Victoria Victorian Hall, where in 1882, the novelist Charles Dickens survived the fall of a plaster cornice. Nearer the Lagan, numbers 38-42 where where veterinary surgeon John Dunlop invented the pneumatic tyre. Ahead, lie St George's Market, the Royal Courts of Justice, the Waterfront Hall and the river.

A less that Titanic stroll would take the visitor from the Memorial at City Hall down past May Street's Georgian tributary thoroughfares, to St George's, the last remaining of a series of dedicated almost riparian Markets, the cereal, the avian, the piscine, the bovine, the porcine and the ovine, these last creatures alone remembered in sculptor Deborah Brown's fine bronze flock herded outside the city's popular concert venue, the perceptively landscaped environment of the Waterfront Hall downstream of which is moored the culturally themed motor vessel Confiance, the French for 'confident' on the newly titled Lanyon Quay. Ross Wilson's sculpted cooper seems lifeless by comparison but Vivien Burnside's

downstream draughtsman's 'Dividers' speak more poignantly of the past, as does Rachel Joynt's pavement sculpture 'Starboard' on the riverside walks. Now the elegantly massy bulk of the Royal Courts of Justice, plus the stylish Bar Library with its doors rich in Irish literary quotations, have replaced the Potato Market where now be-wigged barristers ruffle the Dickensian miasmas of Jarndyce and Jarndyce.

But Belfast's most loved icon is, without doubt, situated on the left bank of the Lagan on Donegal Quay close to the Weir, the Lagan Boat Company's berth, the Lagan Bus Centre and the Custom House. Devised by Professor John Kindness, it is a vast and amusing 'Big Fish', a vast 'salmon of knowledge' whose ceramic scales recount, fetchingly, the city's histories.

North of May's Meadows and the off-city centre Central (Railway) Station, is this weighty-looking Albert Bridge, dating from 1890 and designed by the City Surveyor, J. C. Bretland to replace its predecessor, a bridge of the same name, which had suffered a collapse. The first bridge here, named the Halfpenny from the toll paid to cross it, had five arches and dated from 1831. With the Improvement Act of 1847 Belfast Corporation bought the structure and it became known as the Albert following the naming of the Queen's Bridge in 1847. Two of its five arches collapsed, dramatically, overnight, in September 1886.

The foundation stone of this new Albert Bridge, named for Queen Victoria's Consort, was laid by her grandson Albert Victor, Duke of Clarence, a 'dissipated' prince of what the political mandarins of the day regarded as an unsavoury sexuality. He had both been blackmailed by two female Whitechapel prostitutes and involved with an insalubrious rent boys scandal involving a Cleveland Street London brothel in 1889, the year he came to Belfast.

Conspiracy theorists branded him as the real Jack the Ripper, a murderous psychopath blamed, but never arrested, for the murder and sexual mutilation of five prostitutes, Polly Nicholls, Annie Chapman, 'Long' Liz Stride, Kate Eddowes and Mary Kelly in foggy gas-lit Whitechapel in the 1880s. Albert wasn't the only suspect; others included the poet Francis Thompson, the painter Walter Sickert and an assortment of barbers' surgeons and pox doctors. But the prince's sexual appetites, his ability to deal surgically with animals he shot for game, plus a plethora of red herrings spread by the royals' secret services meant that the suspicion which grew like wildfire, was flaunted in a number of horror movies, novels and plays.

Others reckoned that Albert fathered a child out of wedlock, that he had gonorrhoea and died of syphilis. A third group obstinately persist that he survived till 1920, sectioned, either in an Isle of Wight asylum, or under close guard in Glamis

GILLIAN LYTTON

The Albert Bridge

Castle, both restrictions to prevent his any possibility of his succession to the throne. Certainly he never became, as was once intended, Viceroy of Ireland. It was, after all, Queen Victoria who had described him, in a letter to one of her daughters, as 'dissipated'.

None of these matters were embraced by the city's press of the time and indeed the *Belfast News Letter*, the oldest continuously published English language daily paper in the world, decreed that, as two telephone tubes and one telegraph cable were incorporated in the Albert Bridge's construction that 'the connection between the city and Ballymacarrett has been carefully looked after'.

Downstream comes the uncomplicated Lagan Railway Bridge, built by Randal, Palmer and Tritton in 1976 at the time of the creation of the new railway station as a replacement of an earlier structure which looked so much like the product of a Hornby model train kit. It had been built, over the years from 1870 till 1875 by Telford McNeill, son of the great railway engineer. A pedestrian walk-way was later added to the downstream side of the current railway bridge.

But it is, confusingly, to the western bank of the Lagan, just downstream of the Lagan Weir that you'll look for Albert Square, flanked by Lanyon's Custom House, and occupying what was known, variously as the Limekiln Dock, Patrick's

Dock and the Salt Pan Dock of 1767, where dockside kilns, established at the salt-pans, burnt lime as part of a rock-salt manufacturing process.

Down stream of the Waterfront the Lagan's riverside walks lead downstream past the Royal Courts of Justice to, in turn, the various urban bridges, namely the Lagan Railway, Queen's, Queen Elizabeth II, plus the pedestrianised Lagan Weir and the motorway and railway preambles of the Dargan/ Lagan Bridge, all heading across the river to proportionally Protestant east-Belfast with its shipyards, its Conn O'Neill bridge at Abetta Parade over the Conn's Water, another Lagan tributary arising in the Castlereagh Hills and entering the mouth of the river via a tidal creek at Victoria Park. Here too are the riparian entertainment malls of the Odyssey Pavilion and the adjoining educational diversions of W5 along Queen's Road on its way past the Samson and Dehlila cranes, the Paint Hall film studios, Harland & Wolff's Drawing Hall, the Royal Navy Volunteer Reserve's HMS Caroline by Alexandra Wharf and the Northern Ireland Science Park, amid the ever-changing, currently being gentrified acres upon acres of the 'Titanic Quarter'. The 'Nomadic', the Titanic's tender, restored and welcoming, is moored beside the Titanic Experience by the Abercorn Basin. But the current focus of the 'Titanic Trail' is the vast Thompson Dry-Dock whose massive horned riveted steel Gate, which was hauled into and out of locking position by massive chains powered by a three cylinder brass hauling engine in less than seven minutes, is itself a masterpiece of Edwardian engineering. Olympic Class Liners once filled the dock's enormous length while its Pump House (now labelled the Thompson Pump-house Visitor Experience), which housed both the Deputy Harbour Master downstairs and the hydraulic-engineers upstairs, also houses the 40ft pump-well via which, using the power of three 1,000hp engines, could pump the dock dry of its 23 million gallons of seawater in around 100 minutes.

The Thompson Dock, 850 to 887ft long, 100ft wide at its bottom and 128ft wide at its coping, is 96ft deep and was the world's largest when it welcomed the building of, first RMS Olympic, then the Britannic and then the Titanic. Named for Robert Thompson, Chairman of the Harbour Commissioners its capstans and hawsers are original and there are plans for the Ulster Folk & Transport Museum to restore its unique steam cranes.

Closer to the main channel, but still on Queen's Island, previously known as Dargan's Island till it was renamed for Queen Victoria's in 1849, two years before housing Belfast's astounding Crystal Palace which had opened in 1851 only to be lost to a fire five years later, lies Alexandra Graving Dock, where those parts of the ships which were normally under water could be assessed. Now permanently flooded and its gates removed, and owing its name to the naval term 'to grave' or

GILLIAN LUTTON

clean a ship's bottom by burning off its accumulated detritus before re-tarring, this dock, was opened on May 21st 1889 by Prince Albert Victor, the grandson her Victorious Majesty deemed 'dissipated', on a visit where his duties also included 'laying' the foundation stone for the Albert Bridge. It is 850ft long and 50ft wide in the base and 63ft wide at the coping.

Moored in the dock, in secure circumstances, lies the Light Cruiser HMS Caroline, built in 1914, the first with geared turbines and powered, according to circumstances by either oil or coal. Now the second oldest commissioned ship in the Royal Navy (the first is Nelson's Flag ship, HMS Victory at Portsmouth), and indeed the sole WWI warship still afloat, Caroline gained her honours at the Battle of Jutland in 1916. Currently the home of the province's Royal Naval Reserve, she can, on occasion, be hired for worthy social functions and arts festival launches.

The Queen's Bridge crossing has a much longer heritage. Its first predecessor was a ford, its second was the Long Bridge, a massive masonry construction built in 1682 of twenty-one arches stretching twenty feet wide and some 2,562 feet in length over the Lagan. It has been aptly credited as being the city's raison d'etre. But the passage of Duke of Schomberg's heavy cannon, bound for the support of King William at the Battle of the Boyne took its toll on this elegant structure, weakening seven of its arches so that they later collapsed when rammed by a ship two years later.

Repaired, and when the 'dead sections' were taken into account, the whole edifice stretched for almost a mile and it was in the 1759 described as, 'the mall where all the company of Belfast take the air of a summer's evening'. Those repairs served their purpose till 1841 when construction began of the Queen's Bridge, built of Newry granite to designs by Sir Charles Lanyon and built by Francis Ritchie at a cost of £27,000 borrowed from the Board of Public Works. Local historians credit the cut-boulder at the Mountpottinger, Albertbridge and Castlereagh crossroads as being both a stone from the Long Bridge and also King William's mounting block.

J.C. Bretland, that busy Corporation surveyor, cantilevered the once truly chaste and commanding bridge widthwise by adding a footpath plus the splendidly decorated ornamental lamp posts which were cast at George Smith's Glasgow Sun Foundry, in 1885.

The Queen Elizabeth Bridge, built of reinforced concrete and dating from the 1960s is purely functional. Not so the Lagan Weir whose four deep piers conceal a series of magical echoey submarine spaces, miniature squash courts as it were, which host dazzling mystical and mythical arts performances.

Rusting Relics,
Shipyard Steam
Cranes

GILLIAN WOTTON

East Belfast, with its challenging Engine Room Gallery and Creative Exchange, is also rich in memories of – and a statue to – the Christian apologist C.S. Lewis author of the Narnia Chronicles, plus Cyprus Avenue a source of bluesman Van Morrison's several hits, plus Stormont's Northern Ireland Assembly, George Best City of Belfast Airport, and, further out along Belfast Lough's right bank, the wonderful Ulster Folk and Transport Museum at Cultra, past Holywood.

Rivers have always run through Belfast. Indeed, even till the late 19th century sections of the Farset could be seen flowing down into the Lagan along what is now High Street and Queen's Square. Reproductions of antique prints showing a tidy and romanticised forest of the mast of ships moored opposite St George's Parish Church may be bought in the Linen Hall, this island's oldest subscription Library whilst original prints might go on sale in Danny Clarke's Ross's Auction Rooms in May Street. Indeed the choir boys at the Chapel at the Ford, St George's predecessor, were paid, in part, in a proportion of the salmon they caught beside the ford which crossed the Farset, the sandy ford, the Béal Feirste in Irish, which gave the city its name.

St George's, a charmingly plain preaching house - which replaced the medieval 'chapel of the ford' – was originally named for King George III, but was consecrated ultimately, for the saint, was designed, superbly, by John Bowden architect of Dublin's Pepper-pot Church, St Stephen's, to be placed behind the admirable portico ferried from the dismantled Ballyscullion House, once home to the Earl-Bishop of Derry. Skipper Street, opposite recalls the captains' lodgings, just as nearby Telford's bistro retains its ship's chandlers looks. Sir James Murray, inventor of Milk of Magnesia, lived near High Street's crossing of Bridge Street. Diagonally across Queen's Square towards Donegall Quay, with, amongst its distinguishing points are a fun-palace of fountains, plus, in interlocked Albert Square, the contrasting solemnity of the last of Francis Anderson Calder, Commander RN's ten water-troughs which provided succour for beasts departing the markets or doomed for the abattoir. 'A righteous man regardeth the life of his beasts' runs his inscription. Both thought-worthy devices outweigh the kitsch of Thanksgiving Square's 'Loopy Lady' as the redbrick city's wits have called her.

Queen's Square also has McHugh's, a public house which claims to be the city's oldest building having though subsumed both La Rue Plumet and Madame Dubarry's, two of Prince's Street's many houses of easy virtue whose workforce which pleasured matelots and judges while 'Professor' Gilbert Spencer, the great painter Stanley's brother, played barrel-house piano to the pounding of bedsprings. Off High Street stands Belfast's repost to Pisa's leaning Tower, the Albert Memorial, notably out of plumb.

Out of line also was the direction of the competition to choose the designer of this memorial to the late Prince Consort. Architect W.J. Barre was, first and then ultimately, its designer. But in between the General Committee reversed their first findings, announcing that, on consideration, the contract should go to instead Lanyon, Lynn and Lanyon, a consideration which had to be reversed again by the outrage occasioned by the discovery that Sir Charles himself, now one of the town's MPs, had been present during the decisive discussions.

Featured, distantly, in Carol Reed's magnificent film *Odd Man Out* much of which was filmed in a replica of the magnificent National Trust owned and preserved Crown Liquor Saloon opposite the splendid Grand Opera House, the four-sided tower is known locally as the Albert Clock. It's octagonal spire, topped with a crown and a weathercock, reaches 113 feet high buttressed by crowned lions and proffering a statue by Samuel Ferres Lynn, fashioned to the likeness of Prince Albert of Saxe-Coburg-Gotha in his garter robes. This Wexford sculptor's 'Black Man', the polemical figure of the Rev Henry Cooke complete with his flowing doctoral robes, so long commanded College Square East, to his west the Royal Belfast Academical Institution set against the city's hills, to his east the view down Wellington Place and Chichester Street to the Waterfront Hall and the Lagan.

Recently wonderfully and physically refurbished and then re-marketed as the focus for 'Old Year's Night' merriment's, the Albert also faces Sir Charles Lanyon's reassuring single-storey Portland stone, Doric and Ionic columned 1852 Northern Bank, now extended and renamed for another banking company. Downstream, along Victoria Street stands Heyn & Sons, Thomas Jackson's ornate sandstone 1863 offering, the town's first purpose-built insurance office, once opposite the Corn Exchange, now the Northern Bank. Upstream lie Lytle and McCausland's marvellous warehouses designed by architect William Hastings in 1867, now the elegant Malmaison Hotel, its interior fashionably crepuscular, is exterior still lavishly decorated with the fine sculptures by Thomas Fitzpatrick. The former Lytle's warehouse is flush with grotesque heads protruding their tongues over the third floor windows and a veritable menagerie of frogs, tortoises, squirrels and exotic birds amongst the rainforest plants on the ground floor. Its rival, once McCausland's, boasts references to the five continents with which the firm would trade, sailing to and fro from Belfast's Lagan docks, namely an African negro, a turbaned Asian, an Oceanic female, an American 'red Indian' and a European Victorian gent, complete with his Dundreary whiskers.

High Street, which now covers the final course of the Farset and its docks, is braced, north and south, with a wen of narrow but enticing entries whose numbers decrease with every development but whose shadows are pickled with the descendants of ancient public bars and oyster house pubs where, it will be claimed, the United Irishmen plotted equality, fraternity and liberty with every quaff. Indeed some of the entries are but a dead end or a broken dogleg, like Cole's Alley, from Church Lane to Ann Street.

But battered as it was by the German Luftwaffe's 1941 blitz bombing, Cole's should have a place in every history. For here was born, to Sarah Mellon, wardrobe-mistress to Kena's Strolling Players, (thespians on the boards at The Vaults round the corner in Ann Street, then called Bridge Street for the neighbouring Long Bridge) and to Lieut. Mathew Mellon of the Madras Infantry, on the 11th of November 1777, a daughter Harriott who, an actress of glowing beauty, would become, for ten years, the mistress of Thomas Coutts, London's richest banker. Thomas, after the death of his first wife, married her not once but twice, in 1815. She was thirty-seven, he seventy nine.

They'd first met when she'd played Lydia Languish in Irish playwright Richard Brinsley Sheridan's comedy 'The Rivals' in London's Drury Lane. Coutts' mercenary daughters – and their husbands – were outraged but otherwise Thomas was a happy man who, in his will in 1882 left Harriott the whole of his vast fortune and his partnership in Coutts Bank.

An adept at banking she was much admired by the author Sir Walter Scott but nevertheless lampooned by 'the old order', perhaps more for her philanthropy than anything else. She married William Aubrey de Vere Beauclerk, ninth duke of St Albans when he was a rather simple-minded twenty-six and she a dazzling forty-nine. It was an exchange of wealth and beauty for nought but title as was, and still is, the custom of the aristocracy. On her death, 6th August 1837, she left most of her fortune to her husband on condition he shared none of it with his rapacious brothers, plus £1.8 million to Angela Georgina Burdett-Coutts, Thomas Coutts youngest grand-daughter, who went on to become the Victorian Age's greatest philanthropist. And all from modest Cole's Alley.

Queen's Square itself was, till the 17th century, where the Belfast river, named the Farset, entered the Lagan: 'Marchants kye' stood to the north, 'George's kye' - named for Black George McCartney whose son Isaac had developed the slob land to the south. This last later took the title of Hanover Quay whilst Marchants became first Chichester, then Gregg's Quay called so by Thomas Greg who built the 320ft dockside on land bought from the Marquis of Donegal's family. Coal boats tied up here, thus the name changed to Coal Quay till the waterway was filled in just before Queen Victoria's visit in 1849. Strickland Lowry's well-known and excellently composed 1765 portrait of Greg and his family is a splendid if unsubtle depiction of provincial wealth.

Interlocking with Queen's Square, eponymous Custom House Square takes its name from the establishment built to be the city's finest public building, one of golden sandstone whose entrance originally faced the river, not the Square. Designed by Lanyon and Lynn, it replaced, in 1857, the Ballast Office of 1790 which had been erected over Daniel Mussenden's reclaimed salt-pans where whiting and cod 'were caught in abundance by line'. Built of Glasgow freestone in the Italiante style the Custom House's original riparian entrance's pediment displays Thomas Fitzpatrick's fine carvings of Neptune with anchor and dolphin, plus Mercury with a sheaf of corn, flanking Britannia with her trident braced by lion and unicorn. Below, the windows' spandrels depict the winged figures of Industry, Commerce, Peace and Manufacture.

William Allingham, a Ballyshannon man educated at Belfast's Academical Institution, worked in the Custom House and wrote, famously, in 1849:

> *Up the airy mountain*
> *Down the rushy glen*
> *We daren't go a-hunting*
> *For fear of little men*

The building was at first more than a Custom House, enclosing as it did the Stamp Offices, the Inland Revenue and the Government Emigration department. No doubt the English novelist Anthony Trollope – an author with almost an obsession with English bishops who worked in the Post Office within the Custom House till he left in 1859, might have been amused that his new entrance steps would someday become a Speaker's Corner from which Arthur Trew, leader of the Belfast Protestant Association and an uncle of John Trew, the News Letter's youngest editor, denounced the Church of Ireland's Bishop of Raphoe for being "as full of Fenianism as an egg is full of meat".

For the non-sectarian dreams – inspired by the storming of the Bastille and the French Revolution in 1792, plus the war for America's Independence – of the mainly middle class, mainly Presbyterian, members of the late 18th century Society of United Irishmen of Belfast who'd met in Peggy Barclay's tavern in Crown Entry off High Street, and in Peggy's other inn in Sugar House Entry running from High Street into Waring Street had, evidently, come to nought. At the time Belle Martin, Peggy's serving girl, having betrayed them, their properties were destroyed and their newspaper, *The Northern Star*, wrecked in a ruthless suppression which thought little of their singing the 'Marseillaise'. Henry Joy McCracken, their leader had been caught and hung at the corner of High Street and Cornmarket over land given to the town by his great-great-grandfather.

Today the city's freshly dubbed 'Cathedral Quarter' – once Belfast's Fleet Street – is rich in boho bars, bistros and bodegas. Encircled by the Lagan to the east and by North, High and York streets to landward, it boasts a veritable Cathedral (St. Anne's, Donegall Street) of galleries: Donegall Street's Belfast Exposed, John Hewitt, Open Window, Paragon, Safehouse and Studio C; Cotton Court's Belfast Print Workshop; Gordon Street's Circus School; Great Patrick Street's Switchroom-Golden Thread; Hill Street's White Room; Lanyon Quay's Gilmore and Waterfront and York Street's Uni. There's also NVTV's community studio off Donegall Street, plus a theatre in an old bank (the Northern), another in a black space complete with boho bistro (Black Box, Hill Street), artists' studios (College of Art & Paragon, Donegall Street), public art (Paddy McCann's, Dunbar Street plus the world's most expensive cocktail (Merchant Hotel, Waring Street), plus its own festival The Cathedral Quarter Arts Festival, which follows on April's Belfast Film Festival to open each May Day in concert with the city's Festival of Fools, followed by Young at Art's Writers' Square Belfast Childrens' Festival. CQAF's sure-fire winner each year is a Van Morrison Lagan boat trip.

The stately offices of the Belfast Harbour Commissioners with its octagonal campanile, has a rather grand Public Room which may be, with the right connections, hired for such agreeable diversions as Belfast poet Michael Longley's

GILLIAN LYTTON

The Custom House

investiture as Ireland Professor of Poetry and for chamber concerts by Lurgan-born internationally renowned pianist Barry Douglas's Camerata Ireland chamber orchestra, contain many other treasures. Chief amongst these for some will be the view from the Board Room over Clarendon Dock and the captain's table commissioned for, but never transported onto, the Titanic. Others would plump for *A Military Procession in Belfast in Honour of Lord Nelson* the most important picture painted by the English artist Thomas Robinson who'd lived perviously, in 1793 at Laurencetown and then in Lisburn where hispatron was Dr Percy, Bishop of Dromore. He also painted *The Battle of Ballynahinch* before moving to Belfast in 1801 where, in 1804 he began his grandiose and dramatic work.

Originally it was intended to represent a 'Review of the Belfast Volunteers and Yeomanry by the Earl of Hardwicke, Lord Lieutenant in 1804' with at least 300 portraits of those – and their ladies – who paid a guinea to be included. The finances of the Marquess of Donegall, the presumed purchaser, were in ruins and so when it did not sell, the artist replaced its Donegal Place background with an idealised and fictional view containing a statue of the hero Lord Nelson, a grand mariner who never visited Belfast. Six feet by nine, the finished work is crowded with the portraits of the town's gentry, plus of Robinson, his wife and his son Tom who later presented the unsold wonder to the Harbour Commissioners. Thomas also

produced a much lauded view of the Giant's Causeway, plus *Two Views of Belfast.*

Planned as the Mariners' Church but established in the main by the Sinclairs as a memorial to one of their family, Sinclair Seamen's Presbyterian Church, with its Italiante campanile tower linked to the main building by an arcaded flying buttress will be, by now, to readers of this book, immediately recognisable as the work of Lanyon, Lynn and Lanyon. However the surprise is its interior devised in nautical fashion by its early 20th century minister, the Reverend Samuel Cochrane, BA, RN, a naval man much influenced by his own experiences and conscious that the building's predecessor was Pilot Street's interdenominational chapel, Bethel, financed by the Seamen's Friendly Society. One of Cochrane's previous incumbents had been the Rev Henry Carson, a noted tippler who promised the church's Elders the denial of all alcohol 'except as ordered by his medical advisor.'

Cochrane's interior incorporates models of ships, lighthouse and an aeroplane, a 'flying boat' suspended from the ceiling, plus brass memorials in the shapes of ships' anchors and ships' wheels. A ships bell, recovered from HMS Hood sounds the service's commencement, the passing of collection boxes in the shape of ships' lifeboats precedes its finish whilst a stained glass window showing the tugboat Maggie at the Queen's Bridge diverts the less holy. The text on the

Harbour Commissioner's
Office and Sinclair
Seamans' Church

porch door which reads 'A Merry Heart Doeth Good Like a Medicine' is a memorial to the Rev Cochrane's father whilst the urn atop the font, itself formerly a ship's binnacle, is inscribed to his 'Mother'.

A little chrome-plated torch, delicately engraved, explains that it once flashed the SOS off St John's Point in 1938 saving the lives of its ship's crew. The pitch-pine pulpit's lectern echoes the curves of a ship's prow, bowsprit and the figurehead from the good ship Mizpah and is flanked, with a little prayer perhaps for the Rev Carson's little problem, by the chronometers and navigation lights salvaged from a Guinness barge.

Corporation Square, a vista named not for the City Corporation but for the 'Corporation for the preservation and improvement of the Port and Harbour of Belfast', later the Harbour Board, was previously Ritchie's Dock named for William Ritchie, Belfast's first major shipbuilder whose firm launched Ireland's first steamship here. Direct Wine Shipments, in a warehouse built in 1860 the same year as nearby Muldoon's Bar, is Kevin McAlinden's family firm, standing opposite the Church.

Clarendon Docks have a splendid history, No.1 Graving Dock having been built by Ritchie from 1796 onwards for the Ballast Board, No. 2 Dry Dock (1826) by another Scotsman David Logan who'd worked on the Bell Rock Lighthouse

and Donaghadee Harbour, and Clarendon itself, a massive 'wet dock' off the Lagan in 1851. Restored, with their related buildings by Ferguson & McIlveen in 1991 for the Laganside Corporation, their surroundings of rough-hewn cobbles, their massive lock gates and their steep downwards flights of stone steps, make them one of the Lagan's most impressive industrial icons

At right angles to the Lagan's flow, west of 'Sailortown' and 'Little Italy', dockside communities survive only through the names of Ship, Shipbuoy, Marine and Pilot Streets, since replaced by a soulless spaghetti of urban motorway. Clifton Street runs up the hill between the red brick terraces of Protestant Shankill and Roman Catholic Ardoyne. Here a Peace-wall, the post-Troubles peace not withstanding, still divides the creeds in an area where 20,000 mainly Catholic worked the linen mills, an industry remembered in the names Flax and Cambrai Streets plus the Conway and Flax Mills, now both artists's studios. Shipbuilding was a mid-19th century arrival, the time when steam-powered linen weaving reigned supreme. But in the 1790s it was the water from the Lagan's Antrim's basalt escarpment's tributaries, the Mile Water, the Farset, the Colin, the Blackstaff, the Clowney and the Forth which powered the tiny cotton mills of Smithfield, Peter's Hill and Carrick Hill. Down's Lagan tributaries, Purdy's Burn and Conn's Water had lesser hills to flow from and thus lesser power. Flooding was constant into the 20th century with the

Blackstaff tidal up to the Boyne Bridge, a crossing formerly known as the Saltwater Bridge on Sandy Row and the Lagan itself only sweet water above Stranmillis, which takes its name from *an Sruthán Millis*, the Sweet Stream.

Thus, a river, the Lagan, which has arisen on the windy slopes of Slieve Croob, passes through it, the city of Belfast, debouching into Belfast Lough. But whom amongst you who is not a geographer will delineate where the river ends and the lough begins? For neither stands, or indeed flows, without the other.

The incursive indentation of the lough afforded Belfast's harbour its earliest protection, offering, for instance, William III's many ships a safe harbour while he engaged both Bangor and Carrickfergus. Indeed so large was his fleet that Samuel Mulleneux, who kept a journal of the King's Irish campaign, described the masts to 'be like a wood' upon the Lough.

In those times privateers took advantage of the Lough's shelter so that merchants shipping tobacco into Belfast awaited at Larne till they could be assured the waters were clear of marauding pirates. Smaller ships of maybe 30 to 40 tons, serving the English and Scottish trade, could sail right up to the Belfast docks whilst larger vessels transferred their cargoes to shallower draught boats, off Holywood, over the deep Pool of Garmoyle. So, with a lack of big ships docking, Belfast's

port's facilities remained relatively primitive till well into the 18th century.

Carrickfergus retains its Anglo-Norman Castle, its Elizabethan parish church, boasting skewed chancel and nave, a leper window and stained glass depicting St Nicholas as Santa Claus. The town's assizes of 1711 witnessed Ireland's last witchcraft trial; a ghost, allegedly, haunts Dobbin's Inn. Whitehead, its arcane promenade the Lough's northernmost point, houses the Railway Preservation Society of Ireland.

Looking across the Lough, from Carrickfergus south to Kinnegar, 'Rabbit Warren' perhaps in Irish, Julius McCullough Lecky Craig, Ulster's William McGonagall, gave verse to the Lough's romance when he, reportedly, wrote:

> *On Carrick's shore I stood an' stood*
> *And looked across till Holywood.*
> *And as I gawped I saw afar*
> *My true love on the Kinnegar.*

> *My love he is a brave young man*
> *Who lives on Carrick's hill*
> *An' if you give him eggs an' ham*
> *He's the boy who'll eat his fill.*

This Lagan book began with a plaintive song, as does many an Ulster evening. So, what better way to end it than with the much jollier Lagan song *The Cruise of the Callabar.*

Come all y'dryland sail-i-ors and listen till me song
It's only forty verses so I won't delay yez long.
It's all about the advent-chi-ors of this oul Lisburn tar,
Who sailed as man before the mast aboard the Callabar.

The Callibar was a clipper ship, well fastened fore and aft.
Her stern stuck out behind her and her helm was a great big shaft.
With half a gale the swell the sail, she made one knot per hour,
She was the fastest ship on the Lagan Canal and only one horse power.

The captain he was a strappin' lad, he stood full four foot two,
His eyes wuz red, his face were green an' his nose was a Prussian Blue,
He wore a leather medal that he won in the Crimea War,
And his wife was steward and passenger cook aboard the Callabar.

One day the captain came to me, he sez, 'Me lad', sez he,
'Would ye like to be a sail-i-or and roam the ragin' sea,
Would ye like to be a sail-i-or on foreign seas to roll?
For we're under orders for Aghalee with half a ton of coal'.

On l'avin the Abercorn basin, the weather it was sublime,
And passing under the oul Queen's Bridge we held the Albert chime,
But goin' up the gasworks straight, a very dangerous part,
We ran aground on a lump of coal that wasn't marked on the chart.

Then all became confus-i-on and stormy winds did blow,
The bo'sun slipped on an orange peel and fell into the hold below.
'More steam, more steam', the captain cried, for we were sorely pressed,
And the engineer, from the bank replied: 'The oul horse is doin' its best'.

When we woke uo next mor-ni-ing, we were in a dreadful funk,
For the mate he'd been drowned dead while sleeping in his bunk.
To stop the ship from sinking and to save each precious life,
We threw all the cargo overboard, includin' the captain's wife.

A farmer on his way to work, he heard us loudly roar,
And he threw us the ends of his gallusses and pulled us all ashore,
So I'm done with ocean ramblin' and roamin' the ragin' main,
And the next time I go to Lisburn, bejabbers I'll go by train!

Angling in Northern Ireland *(undated). Belfast (Tourist Information Centre)*

Angling Guide. *(undated). Belfast (Dept. of Agriculture for Northern Ireland)*

Archaeology Data Service (2008). *http:adsahds.ac.uk*

The Archaeological Survey of Northern Ireland Co. Down.(1966). *Belfast. (H.M.S.O.)*

Ards and Down Area Plan 2015 (20002 draft). *Belfast (Planning Service)*

BARDON, J. (1992) **A History of Ulster**. *Belfast (Blackstaff Press)*

BASSETT, G.H. **(1988) County Down 100 Years Ago: A Guide and Directory 1886.** *Belfast. (Reprint, Friar's Bush Press)*

BAUCHER, J. **(2006) A Look Around Laganside.** *Belfast(www.johnbaucher.com)*

BECKETT, J.C. (et al) **(1983) Belfast The Making of the City.** *Belfast (Appletree Press)*

BEESLEY, S. & WHITE, J. **(1997) Urban Flora of Belfast.** *Belfast (Institute of Irish Studies)*

Belfast Street Map, scale 1:12 000. *Belfast (O.S.N.I)*

Belfast Ultimate Travel Map (2007) *Belfast. (Translink/B.V.C.B.)*

BLACK, E. (2006) **Art in Belfast 1760-1888.** *Dublin (Irish Academic Press)*

BLAIR, M. (2000) **Once Upon The Lagan.** *Belfast (Blackstaff Press)*

BRETT, C.E.B. (1985) **Buildings of Belfast.** *Belfast (Revised, Friar's Bush)*

BRETT, C.E.B. (1996) **Buildings of County Antrim.** *Belfast (U.A.H.S)*

BRETT, C.E.B. (2002) **Buildings of North County Down.** *Belfast (U.A.H.S.)*

BRETT. C.E.B. (2004) **Georgian Belfast, 1750 - 1850.** *Dublin (R. I. Academy)*

CHESNEY, H.C.G. AND FOSTER, J.W. **(1997) Nature in Ireland.** *Dublin (Appletree Press)*

CLARKE, P.J. (2004) **History of a County Down Townland: Drumaroad** *Drumaroad. (Patrick Clarke Publishing)*

CRAIG, P. (ed) (2006) **The Ulster Anthology.** *Belfast (Blackstaff Press)*

CRAWFORD, W.H. (2005) **The Impact of the Domestic Linen Industry in Ulster.** *Belfast (Ulster Historical Foundation)*

COLLINS, B., OLLERENSHAW, P. AND PARKHILL, T. (eds) (2005) **Industry, Trade and People in Ireland.** *Belfast (Ulster Historical Foundation)*

CURL, J.S. (2006) **A Dictionary of Architecture.** *Oxford (O.U.P.)*

DAWSON, K.L. (2008) **Monro, Henry.** *Oxford (O.D.N.B.)*

DAY, A. & McWilliams, P. (eds) **Ordnance Survey Memoirs of Ireland.** *Belfast (Institute of Irish Studies)*

DEAN, J.A.K. (1994) **The Gatelodges of Ulster.** *Belfast (U.A.H.S)*

DELANEY, R. (1986) **Ireland's Inland Waterways.** *Belfast (Appletree Press)*

DEMPSEY, E. & O'CLERY, M. **(2002) Complete Guide to Ireland's Birds.** *Dublin (Gill & Macmillan)*

Dictionary of Irish Terms/Foclóir Téarmalochta (2008) *www.focal.ie*

Discoverer Map Series. Sheets 15 & 20, scale 1: 50 000. *Belfast (O.S.N.I.)*

DIXON, H. (1975 & 2008) **An Introduction to Ulster Architecture.** *Belfast (U.A.H.S.)*

EAVNS, E.E. (1957) **Irish Folk Ways.** *London. (Routledge & Keegan Paul)*

EVANS, R. (1988) **The Visitors' Guide to Northern Ireland.** *Belfast (Blackstaff)*

FENTON, J. (2006) **The Hamely Tongue.** *Belfast (Ullans Press)*

FLANAGAN, D. & FLANAGAN, L. **Irish Place Names.** *Dublin (Gill & Macmillan)*

GALLOWAY, P. (1992) **The Cathedrals of Ireland.** *Belfast (Inst.of Irish Studies)*

GILLESPIE, R. & Royle, S.A. (2003) **BELFAST Part 1, to 1840. Irish Historic Towns Atlas No. 12.** *Dublin (Royal Irish Academy with B.C.C.)*

GILLESPIE, R. (2007) **Early Belfast.** *Belfast (Belfast Natural History and Philosophical Society)*

GREEN, E.R.R., (1963) **The Industrial Archaeology of County Down.** *Belfast (H.M.S.O.)*

HERBERT, S. (ed.) (2007) **TQ Titanic Quarter Regenerating Belfast.** *London (3FoxInternational)*

HILL, I. (1992) **The Fish of Ireland.** *Belfast (Appletree Press)*

HILL, I. et al (2007) **Turning the tide for Belfast.** *Belfast (Laganside Corporation)*

HOLDEN, R. (2004) **Harty, Sir Hamilton.** *Oxford (O.D.N.B.)*

INGAMELLS, J. (2004) **Wallace, Sir Richard.** *Oxford (O.D.N.B.)*

INGAMELLS, J. (1985) **The Wallace Collection Catalogue.** *London (Wallace Collection)*

KISTE, J.V.D. **(2004) Albert Victor, Prince, Duke of Clarence and Avondale.** *Oxford (O.D.N.B.)*

LARMOUR, P. **Lanyon, Sir Charles.** *Oxford (O.D.N.B.)*

LEWIS, S. (1837) **County Down: A Topographical Dictionary of the Parishes, Villages and Towns of County Down.** *Reprint (Friar's Bush Press)*

Lisburn Conservation Area (undated) *(Department of the Environment (NI))*

Listed Buildings (2008) www.ehsni.gov.uk. *Belfast (Environment & Heritage Service)*

LYLE, P. (2003) **Classical Geology, Northern Ireland.** *Harpenden (Terra)*

MACAFEE, C.I. (ed.) (1966) **A Consise Ulster Dictionary.** *Oxford (O.U.P.)*

McCRACKEN, E. (1971) **The Plam House and Botanic Garden.** *Belfast (U.A.H.S.)*

McCUTCHEON, W.A. (1980) **The Industrial Heritage of Northern Ireland.** *Belfast (H.M.S.O.)*

McVEAGH (ed) **(1995 Richard Pococke's Irish Tours.** *Blackrock (Irish Academic Press)*

McKAY, P. (1999) **A Dictionary of Ulster Placenames.** *Belfast (Institute of Irish Studies)*

McKAY P. & MUHR, K. **(2007) Lough Neagh Placenames.** *Belfast (Queen's University)*

McLEOD, S. McC. (ed.) **(Undated) Motoring, golf and angling in Northern Ireland.** *Belfast (T.I.O.)*

MACKEY, B. (2000) **Lisburn The Town and its People 1873-1937.** *Belfast (Blackstaff Press)*

MAGUIRE, W.A. (ed.) **Up in Arms: The 1798 Rebellion in Ireland.** *Belfast (Ulster Museum)*

MARSHALL, P. (2004) **Hill, Wills 1st marquess of Downshire.** *Oxford (ODNB)*

Moira Conservation Area. (undated) *(Department of the Environment (NI))*

Monuments. (2008) *www.ehsni.gov.uk Belfast (Environment & Heritage Service)*

MULVILL, M. (2002) **Ingenious Ireland.** *Dublin (Town House)*

NELSON, E.C. & Walsh, W.F. (1993) **Trees of Ireland.** *Dublin (Lilliput Press)*

PATTON, M (1993) **Central Belfast A Historical Gazetter.** *Belfast (U.A.H.S.)*

PERKIN, J. (2008) **Harriott, duchess of St Albans.** *Oxford (O.D.N.B.)*

PITCHER, J. & HALL, V. **Flora Hibernica: the wild flowers, plants and trees of Ireland.** *Cork (Collins Press)*

PRAEGER, R.L. (1939) **The Way That I Went.** *Dublin (Hodges, Figgis & Co.)*

RANKIN, K. (2002) **The Linen Houses of the Lagan Valley.** *Belfast (Ulster Historical Foundation)*

RITCHIE, R. (2004) **Rawdon [née Hastings], Elizabeth.** *Oxford (O.D.N.B.)*

ROYLE, S.A. (2007) **BELFAST Part II, 1840 - 1900. Irish Historic Towns Atlas No. 17. Dublin** *(Royal Irish Academy with B.C.C.)*

SANDFORD, E. (1976) **Discover Northern Ireland.** *Belfast (NITB)*

SCOTT, R. (2000) **A Breath of Fresh Air: The Story of Belfast Parks.** *Belfast (Blackstaff Press)*

SCOTT, R. (2004) **Wild Belfast: on safari in the city.** *Belfast (Blackstaff Press)*

SIMON, B. (ed) **A Treasured Landscape: The Heritage of Belvoir Park.** *Belfast (The Forest of Belfast)*

STERRY, P. (2004) **Complete Irish Wildlife.** *London (HarperCollins)*

STEVENSON, J. (1990) **Two Centuries of Life in County Down 1600-1800.** *Belfast (White Row Press)*

STEWART, A.T.Q. **The Summer Soldiers: The 1798 Rebellion in Antrim and Down.** *Belfast (Blackstaff)*

Street Atlas Co Armagh, Co Down (2006) 2 2/3in.=1 ml. *London (Philip's)*

Street Atlas Belfast, Antrim, Lisburn (2006) scale ditto (2006) *London (Philip's)*

THOMPSON, R. & NELSON, B. (2006) **The Butterflies and Moths of Northern Ireland.** *Belfast (National Museums of Ireland)*

Titanic Trail (2006) *Belfast (Belfast City Council).*

WILLIAMS, J. (1994) **A Companion Guide to Architecture in Ireland.** *Dublin (Irish Academic Press)*

Dear Reader

This book is from our exciting new range which cover rivers in Ireland and includes:–

By the Banks of the Bann　　　　　　**The Liffey**
My Lagan Love　　　　　　　　　　　**Following the Foyle**

This new range is a development of our much complimented illustrated book series which includes:-

Belfast
By the Lough's North Shore
East Belfast
South Belfast
Antrim, Town & Country
North Antrim
Across the Roe
Inishowen
Donegal Highlands
Donegal, South of the Gap
Donegal Islands
Islands of Connaught
Sligo
Mayo
North Kerry
Fermanagh
Omagh
Cookstown
Dundalk & North Louth
Drogheda & the Boyne Valley
Fingal
Dublin's North Coast

Blanchardstown, Castleknock and the Park
Dundrum, Stillorgan & Rathfarnham
Blackrock, Dun Laoghaire and Dalkey
Bray and North Wicklow
Dublin 4
Limerick's Glory
Galway on the Bay
Connemara
The Book of Clare
Kildare
Carlow
Monaghan
Athlone
Cavan
Kilkenny
Armagh
Ring of Gullion
Carlingford Lough
The Mournes
Heart of Down
Strangford's Shores
Lecale

Cottage
Publications

Cottage Publications
is an imprint of
Laurel Cottage Ltd
15 Ballyhay Road
Donaghadee, Co. Down
N. Ireland, BT21 0NG

For details on these superb publications
and to view samples of the paintings they
contain, you can visit our web site
www.cottage-publications.com
or alternatively you can contact us as
follows:–
Telephone: +44 (0)28 9188 8033
Fax: +44 (0)28 9188 8063

We can also supply prints, individually signed by the artist, of the paintings
featured in many of the above titles as well as many other areas of Ireland.

For the more athletically minded our illustrated walking book series includes:–
Bernard Davey's Mourne　　　　　　　Tony McAuley's Glens
Bernard Davey's Mourne Part 2　　　　Rathlin, An Island Odyssey